# The Avocado Industry: Mexico/United States and the Globe in General

*A Comprehensive Account into the Challenges faced due to the involvement of Violent Cartels and Corruption*

**Vertex Publishing**

Copyright © 2024 Vertex Publishing

All rights reserved. No part of this publication may be reproduced, distributed, or transmitted in any form or by any means, including photocopying, recording, or other electronic or mechanical methods, without the prior written permission of the publisher, except in the case of brief quotations embodied in critical reviews and certain other noncommercial uses permitted by copyright law

Table of Contents

Introduction: The Avocado Industry: An Overview 8
    Economic Significance of Avocados in Mexico and the US..................9
        Mexico: The World's Avocado Powerhouse 10
        United States: A Major Consumer and Producer..................10
        Challenges and Opportunities..................11
    The Appeal of "Green Gold"..................11
        Nutritional Benefits..................12
        Culinary Versatility..................12
        Economic Value..................12
        Cultural Significance..................13
        Environmental Impact..................13

Chapter 1: The Avocado Journey..................14
    From Orchard to Table: The Lifecycle of an Avocado..................14
        Cultivation and Growth..................14
        Harvesting..................14
        Sorting and Packing..................15
        Distribution..................15
        Ripening and Retail..................15
        Consumption..................16
    Key Regions for Avocado Cultivation..................16
        Mexico: The Heartland of Avocado Production..................16

    California: A Pillar of US Production.......... 17
    Peru: A Rising Star in Avocado Exports...... 17
    Chile: An Established Exporter................... 18
    Other Emerging Regions............................ 18
  The Role of Inspectors in Ensuring Quality......19
    Responsibilities of Avocado Inspectors.......19
    Challenges Faced by Inspectors.................. 20
    Significance of Inspection in the Avocado Industry................................................ 20

## Chapter 2: The Michoacán Connection...................22
  Geographic and Agricultural Overview of Michoacán............................................... 22
    Geographic Features................................. 22
    Climate and Weather................................23
    Agricultural Practices................................23
    Economic Impact........................................ 24
  The Soil and Climate: Why Michoacán is Ideal for Avocados........................................25
    Geographic and Climatic Conditions.......... 25
    Soil Composition......................................... 26
    Agricultural Practices.................................26
  Historical Context: Growth of the Avocado Industry................................................ 27
    Ancient Beginnings....................................27
    Colonial Influence and Early Trade............ 28
    20th Century Expansion............................ 28
    Modern Era and Global Dominance........... 29

- Challenges and Resilience..........................30
- Chapter 3: The Cartel Influence............................ 31
  - The Entry of Cartels into the Avocado Trade....31
    - Origins of Cartel Involvement..................... 31
    - Methods of Cartel Control..........................32
    - Impact on Local Communities and Farmers..32
    - Global Market Implications........................ 33
    - Efforts to Combat Cartel Influence............. 34
  - Mechanisms of Control: Extortion, Corruption, and Violence......................................................35
    - Extortion and Protection Rackets................ 35
    - Corruption and Complicity.......................... 36
    - Violence and Intimidation...........................37
    - Addressing Challenges and Building Resilience.....................................................38
  - Case Studies of Cartel Involvement..................39
    - Case Study 1: The Knights Templar Cartel. 39
    - Case Study 2: The Jalisco New Generation Cartel (CJNG)............................................... 41
    - Case Study 3: Local Cartel Influence and Community Resistance................................42
- Chapter 4: The Crisis..............................................45
  - The Incident: Assault and Detention of US Inspectors..........................................................45
    - Background of the Incident.........................45
    - The Assault and Detention.......................... 45
    - Immediate Repercussions...........................46

- Broader Implications..................................46
- Government and Industry Response..........47
- Long-Term Implications............................48
- Immediate Impacts on Trade and Prices.........49
  - Disruption of Supply Chains......................49
    - Supply Chain Control and Manipulation.. 49
    - Impact on Quality and Consistency...... 50
  - Price Volatility..............................................50
    - Short-Term Price Spikes........................50
    - Long-Term Price Instability...................51
  - Economic Impact on Farmers and Local Communities................................................. 52
    - Financial Strain on Farmers..................52
    - Community Impact................................52
  - International Trade Implications...............53
    - Trade Relations and Policies................. 53
    - Market Diversification........................... 53
- Diplomatic and Economic Repercussions........54
  - Economic Repercussions............................54
    - Market Instability and Price Volatility.. 54
    - Economic Losses and Increased Costs.. 55
    - Impact on Investment and Economic Development........................................... 55
  - Diplomatic Repercussions..........................56
    - Strained Bilateral Relations...................56
    - International Cooperation and Support 57

- Diplomatic Negotiations and Advocacy.57
- Broader Socioeconomic Implications..........58
  - Human Rights and Social Justice...........58
- Environmental Sustainability......................58
- Economic Inequality and Development.......59
- Chapter 5: Regulatory Framework........................ 60
  - Existing Bilateral Agreements and Inspection Protocols............................................................. 60
    - Bilateral Agreements....................................60
      - The 1997 US-Mexico Avocado Trade Agreement................................................60
      - The 2007 North American Free Trade Agreement (NAFTA)............................... 61
      - The 2020 United States-Mexico-Canada Agreement (USMCA).............................. 61
    - Inspection Protocols....................................62
      - USDA Animal and Plant Health Inspection Service (APHIS)....................62
      - Mexican National Service for Agro-Alimentary Public Health, Safety, and Quality (SENASICA).......................63
  - Evolution and Challenges of Inspection Protocols.........................................................63
    - Evolution of Inspection Protocols.......... 63
    - Challenges in Inspection Protocols....... 64
  - The Role of the USDA and APHIS in Avocado Trade.................................................................. 65
    - USDA and APHIS: An Overview................. 65

- Ensuring Pest-Free Imports .......................... 66
- Promoting Safe and Legal Trade .................. 67
- Facilitating International Trade .................. 68
- Addressing Challenges and Future Directions ................................................. 69
- Proposed Changes and Their Implications ...... 70
  - Enhanced Security Measures ...................... 70
    - Increased Protection for Inspectors ....... 70
    - Increased Presence of Law Enforcement .. 71
  - Regulatory and Certification Reforms .......... 71
    - Strengthening Certification Processes ... 71
    - Implementing Traceability Systems ...... 72
  - Environmental and Land Use Policies ........ 72
    - Enforcing Land Use Regulations ........... 73
    - Promoting Reforestation and Conservation ............................................. 73
  - Diplomatic and Trade Policy Adjustments . 74
    - Revising Bilateral Trade Agreements .... 74
    - Supporting International Advocacy and Standards .................................................. 74
- Chapter 6: The Human Element ............................ 76
  - The Lives of Avocado Farmers and Inspectors . 76
    - The Lives of Avocado Farmers ..................... 76
      - Daily Life on the Farm ........................... 76
      - Social and Community Impact ............... 77
      - Success Stories and Aspirations ............. 77

- The Lives of Avocado Inspectors..................78
  - Roles and Responsibilities.....................78
  - Impact on Personal Life........................78
  - Professional Development and Recognition..............................79
- Personal Stories from the Field......................80
  - José's Struggle for Survival.......................80
  - María's Dream of Education......................80
  - Miguel's Fight for Environmental Justice...81
  - Luisa's Hope for Change............................81
- The Risks and Rewards of Working in Michoacán.......................................82
  - Risks.............................................. 82
    - Security Threats and Violence...............82
    - Economic Vulnerability........................83
    - Environmental and Social Challenges...83
  - Rewards........................................84
    - Economic Opportunities and Employment.......................................... 84
    - Market Access and Global Demand...... 84
    - Technological Advancements and Innovation.............................................85
    - Community Development and Social Impact.................................................. 85
- Chapter 7: Environmental Concerns.....................87
  - The Issue of Illegal Deforestation.....................87
    - Causes of Illegal Deforestation...................87
    - Impacts of Illegal Deforestation................87

- Efforts to Address Illegal Deforestation..... 88
- Environmental Impact of Avocado Farming....89
  - Deforestation and Habitat Loss.................. 89
  - Water Resource Management..................... 90
  - Soil Health and Erosion Control................. 90
  - Climate Change Impacts............................. 91
  - Conservation and Sustainable Practices..... 92
- Sustainable Practices and Future Outlook....... 92
  - Current Sustainable Practices..................... 93
    - Conservation of Natural Resources....... 93
    - Biodiversity Conservation..................... 93
  - Social Responsibility and Community Engagement................................................. 94
  - Future Outlook............................................ 94
    - Innovation and Technological Advancements........................................ 94
    - Sustainable Supply Chain Management 95
    - Policy and Regulatory Support.............. 95
- Chapter 8: Solutions and Future Directions.......... 97
  - Strengthening Security and Oversight.............. 97
    - Enhanced Security Measures..................... 97
      - Law Enforcement Collaboration............ 97
      - Community Engagement and Empowerment....................................... 98
    - Regulatory Oversight and Compliance....... 98
      - Strengthening Regulatory Frameworks 98
      - Public-Private Partnerships................... 99

Future Directions........................................... 99
    Innovation and Technology Integration.... 99
    Policy Innovation and Governance...... 100
Technological Innovations in Agriculture and Monitoring......................................................... 100
    Precision Agriculture................................. 101
    Automated Farming Technologies............ 101
    Data-driven Decision Support Systems.... 102
    Future Prospects........................................ 103
International Cooperation and Policy Recommendations......................................... 104
    Importance of International Cooperation. 105
        Trade Relations and Market Access..... 105
        Environmental Sustainability and Conservation............................................ 105
        Social Responsibility and Labor Rights..... 106
    Policy Recommendations.......................... 106
        Strengthening Regulatory Frameworks.... 106
        Promoting Sustainable Supply Chains 107
        Empowering Stakeholder Engagement..... 107

Chapter 9: Consumer Awareness........................ 109
    Understanding the Journey of Your Avocado 109
        The Global Avocado Supply Chain............ 109
        Environmental and Social Considerations 110

- Making Informed Choices.................................110
- Supporting Ethical and Sustainable Practices 111
- Environmental Sustainability......................111
- Social Responsibility and Labor Rights......112
- Supply Chain Transparency and Accountability...............................................113
- Policy and Advocacy....................................113
- Making Informed Choices as a Consumer........114
  - Understanding Sustainability Certifications.. 114
  - Ethical Sourcing Practices...........................115
  - Consumer Behavior and Supply Chain Impact..............................................................115
  - Promoting Positive Change........................116
- Conclusion............................................................117
  - Challenges.....................................................118
  - Opportunities...............................................118
  - Summarizing the Path Forward..................119
- The Future of the Avocado Industry in a Global Context.................................................................119
  - Emerging Trends and Market Dynamics.. 120
  - Technological Innovations and Agricultural Advancements............................................... 120
  - Global Trade Dynamics and Policy Considerations...............................................121
  - Opportunities for Innovation and Market Expansion.......................................................121

# Introduction: The Avocado Industry: An Overview

## The Rise of Avocados in Global Markets

Over the past few decades, avocados have transcended their status as a regional fruit to become a global phenomenon. This rise can be attributed to a combination of their unique nutritional profile, versatility in culinary applications, and effective marketing strategies that have positioned them as a superfood.

**Nutritional Appeal**

Avocados are celebrated for their rich content of healthy fats, vitamins, and minerals. They are particularly high in monounsaturated fats, which are known to promote heart health. Additionally, avocados provide significant amounts of vitamins K, E, C, and B-6, along with folate, magnesium, and potassium. This nutritional density has made them a favorite among health-conscious consumers and nutritionists alike.

**Culinary Versatility**

The creamy texture and mild flavor of avocados lend themselves to a wide variety of dishes, ranging from traditional guacamole to innovative uses in smoothies, salads, and even desserts. This versatility has enabled avocados to seamlessly integrate into diverse cuisines around the world. Food influencers and chefs have played a crucial role in popularizing creative avocado recipes, further boosting their global appeal.

**Marketing and Branding**

The marketing campaigns around avocados have been remarkably successful. Organizations such as the Hass Avocado Board have invested heavily in promoting the health benefits and culinary uses of avocados. Through social media, cooking shows, and health blogs, the message has been clear: avocados are a delicious and nutritious addition to any diet. This strategic branding has helped position avocados as a trendy and desirable fruit.

**Global Production and Trade**

The surge in demand has led to a significant increase in global avocado production. Countries like Mexico, which is the largest producer of avocados, have expanded their cultivation to meet this growing market. Other countries, including the United States, Peru, and Chile, have also become major players in the avocado trade. Advances in agricultural practices and supply chain logistics have made it possible to transport avocados across great distances while maintaining their quality.

**Economic Impact**

The avocado industry's expansion has had profound economic implications. In Mexico, for instance, avocados are a major export product, contributing billions of dollars to the national economy. The increased demand has also created jobs and boosted local economies in various avocado-growing regions. However, this growth has not been without challenges, including environmental concerns and issues related to fair labor practices.

**Challenges and Future Prospects**

Despite its success, the avocado industry faces several challenges. Sustainability is a major concern, as the environmental impact of large-scale avocado farming, including deforestation and water usage, has come under scrutiny. Additionally, the involvement of criminal organizations in some avocado-producing areas poses significant risks to the industry's stability and reputation.

Looking ahead, the industry must address these challenges to ensure its continued growth. Efforts to promote sustainable farming practices, improve supply chain transparency, and enhance security measures are essential. As consumer awareness and demand for ethically produced avocados grow, the industry has the opportunity to innovate and adapt, securing its place in the global market for years to come.

In summary, the rise of avocados in global markets is a testament to their nutritional benefits, culinary flexibility, and effective marketing. While the industry faces notable challenges, its potential for continued growth remains strong, driven by an ever-increasing demand from health-conscious consumers around the world.

# Economic Significance of Avocados in Mexico and the US

The avocado industry has become a cornerstone of economic activity in both Mexico and the United States. As demand for avocados has surged globally, these two countries have positioned themselves as leaders in production and trade, reaping substantial economic benefits.

## Mexico: The World's Avocado Powerhouse

Mexico is the world's largest producer and exporter of avocados, with the state of Michoacán at the heart of this booming industry. The fertile volcanic soil and favorable climate conditions make Michoacán an ideal location for avocado cultivation, leading to its dominance in global markets.

**Economic Impact:**
- **Revenue Generation:** In 2023, Mexico exported approximately 2.2 million metric tons of avocados, generating an estimated $2.7 billion in revenue. This substantial

income supports a wide range of economic activities, from farming to logistics.
- **Employment:** The avocado industry is a significant employer in Mexico. It provides jobs for over 300,000 people directly involved in cultivation, harvesting, processing, and transportation. Additionally, it creates indirect employment opportunities in related sectors such as packaging, marketing, and export services.
- **Rural Development:** Avocado farming has played a crucial role in the economic development of rural areas in Michoacán and other avocado-growing regions. The industry's growth has led to improved infrastructure, better access to services, and increased standards of living for many communities.

## United States: A Major Consumer and Producer

While Mexico dominates production, the United States stands out as the largest consumer of avocados. The demand for avocados in the US has skyrocketed over the past two decades, driven by the fruit's popularity in health-conscious diets and diverse culinary applications.

**Economic Impact:**
- **Import Market:** The US imports over 80% of its avocados from Mexico. This import activity is a critical component of the US-Mexico trade relationship, with avocados representing a significant share of agricultural imports. The consistent demand ensures a steady flow of revenue for Mexican exporters and reliable supply chains for US distributors.
- **Domestic Production:** California, Florida, and Hawaii are key avocado-producing states in the US. Although domestic production is much smaller than imports, it still contributes significantly to the local economies. California, in particular, is renowned for its high-quality avocados, with the industry generating over $400 million annually.
- **Retail and Food Service:** The US retail and food service sectors have capitalized on the avocado craze. From grocery stores to restaurants, the fruit's popularity drives sales and menu innovations. Avocado-based products such as guacamole have become

staples, further enhancing the economic value of avocados.

## Challenges and Opportunities

Despite its economic benefits, the avocado industry faces several challenges:
- **Sustainability:** The environmental impact of large-scale avocado farming, including deforestation and water use, poses sustainability concerns. Efforts are underway to promote more sustainable farming practices to ensure long-term viability.
- **Security and Stability:** The influence of cartels and associated violence in regions like Michoacán disrupts the stability of the industry. Enhancing security measures and addressing corruption are crucial for safeguarding the industry's future.

The economic significance of avocados in Mexico and the US cannot be overstated. The industry's contributions to revenue generation, employment, and rural development highlight its importance. Addressing the challenges will be essential to maintain and grow the economic benefits derived from this valuable commodity, ensuring that both producers and consumers continue to enjoy the fruits of their labor.

## The Appeal of "Green Gold"

Avocados, often referred to as "green gold," have become a staple in diets worldwide, symbolizing health, wealth, and culinary versatility. The allure of this creamy, nutrient-rich fruit extends beyond its taste, making it a sought-after commodity in global markets. This chapter explores the multifaceted appeal of avocados and why they have earned their illustrious nickname.

### Nutritional Benefits

One of the primary reasons for the avocado's popularity is its exceptional nutritional profile. Avocados are rich in healthy monounsaturated fats, which contribute to heart health by lowering bad cholesterol levels. They are also packed with vitamins and minerals, including vitamin K, vitamin E, vitamin C, and various B vitamins. Additionally, avocados provide a significant amount of potassium, more than bananas, which is essential for maintaining healthy blood pressure levels.

The high fiber content in avocados supports digestive health and contributes to a feeling of fullness, making them a popular choice for those looking to maintain or lose weight. The presence of antioxidants, such as lutein and zeaxanthin, also promotes eye health by protecting against age-related macular degeneration.

## Culinary Versatility

The creamy texture and mild flavor of avocados make them a versatile ingredient in a variety of culinary applications. They can be used in both savory and sweet dishes, from the classic guacamole to avocado toast, smoothies, salads, and even desserts like avocado chocolate mousse. This versatility has helped avocados become a beloved ingredient in cuisines around the world.

Avocados' ability to enhance the nutritional profile of meals without overpowering other flavors makes them a favorite among chefs and home cooks alike. Their unique texture allows them to be used as a healthy substitute for butter or oil in baking, adding moisture and richness without the added saturated fats.

## Economic Value

The economic impact of avocados, particularly in Mexico, cannot be overstated. As the world's largest producer of avocados, Mexico's economy benefits significantly from the export of this fruit. The global demand for avocados has created a robust industry that supports thousands of jobs, from farming and harvesting to transportation and sales.

In regions like Michoacán, where the majority of Mexico's avocados are grown, the fruit is a vital source of income for local communities. The lucrative nature of the avocado market has led to increased investment in agricultural technology and infrastructure, further boosting the industry's economic significance.

## Cultural Significance

Beyond their nutritional and economic value, avocados hold cultural significance in many parts of the world. In Mexico, avocados have been cultivated for thousands of years and are deeply embedded in the country's culinary traditions. They are celebrated during festivals and are a symbol of Mexican heritage and pride.

In other parts of the world, avocados have become synonymous with modern, health-conscious lifestyles. The rise of social media has further propelled their popularity, with avocado-based dishes frequently featured in food blogs, Instagram posts, and cooking shows. This cultural trend has solidified avocados' status as a symbol of healthy living and contemporary cuisine.

## Environmental Impact

While the appeal of avocados is undeniable, it is also important to consider their environmental impact. The growing demand for avocados has led to concerns about deforestation, water usage, and sustainability practices in avocado farming. Efforts are being made to address these issues through sustainable farming practices, certifications, and regulations to ensure that the growth of the avocado industry does not come at the expense of the environment.

The appeal of "green gold" lies in its comprehensive benefits—nutritional, culinary, economic, and cultural. As the global demand for avocados continues to rise, it is crucial to balance this growth with sustainable practices to ensure that the allure of this beloved fruit can be enjoyed for generations to come.

# Chapter 1: The Avocado Journey

## From Orchard to Table: The Lifecycle of an Avocado

The journey of an avocado from the orchard to the dining table is a complex process that involves multiple stages of cultivation, harvesting, and distribution. This chapter delves into each step of the avocado's lifecycle, highlighting the meticulous care and coordination required to bring this nutritious fruit to consumers worldwide.

### Cultivation and Growth

The lifecycle of an avocado begins with the careful selection of a suitable growing environment. Avocado trees thrive in regions with a mild climate, well-drained soil, and plenty of sunlight. Key regions for avocado cultivation include Mexico, California, Peru, and Chile, each providing the optimal conditions necessary for the fruit to flourish.

Avocado trees are typically propagated through grafting, a process where a scion (a young shoot or twig) from a desired variety is joined to a rootstock. This method ensures that the trees produce fruit with consistent quality and characteristics. Once grafted, the trees are planted in orchards, where they require regular watering, fertilization, and pest control.

The trees take several years to mature and begin producing fruit. During this time, they undergo various growth stages, from flowering to fruit set and development. The flowering stage is particularly critical, as avocado trees are known for their complex pollination process. They have flowers that open twice, first as female and then as male, requiring cross-pollination to ensure fruit set.

## Harvesting

The harvesting phase is a labor-intensive process that demands precision and timing. Avocados do not ripen on the tree; instead, they mature and are harvested when they reach the desired size and oil content. The timing of the harvest is crucial, as picking the fruit too early or too late can affect its quality and shelf life.

Skilled workers, often using specialized poles or clippers, carefully pick the avocados by hand to avoid bruising the delicate fruit. The harvested avocados are then collected in bins and transported to packing facilities. It's essential that this process is done swiftly to maintain the fruit's freshness and quality.

## Sorting and Packing

Once at the packing facility, the avocados undergo a thorough sorting and grading process. They are inspected for size, color, and any signs of damage or defects. This step ensures that only the highest quality avocados make it to market.

The avocados are then cleaned and sorted into different grades based on their size and quality. After sorting, they are packed into cartons or crates designed to protect the fruit during transportation. Proper packing is vital to prevent damage and extend the shelf life of the avocados.

## Distribution

The next phase in the lifecycle is distribution. Packed avocados are loaded onto trucks or shipping containers and transported to various destinations, including domestic markets and international export hubs. The logistics of avocado distribution are complex, involving temperature-controlled environments to maintain the fruit's freshness during transit.

Efficient supply chain management is crucial to ensure that avocados reach retailers and consumers in optimal condition. This includes coordinating transportation schedules, monitoring storage conditions, and managing customs and regulatory requirements for international shipments.

## Ripening and Retail

Upon arrival at their destination, avocados are often sent to ripening facilities where they undergo controlled ripening processes. Ethylene gas is commonly used to regulate the ripening, allowing avocados to reach the perfect stage for consumption when they hit the store shelves.

Retailers play a key role in the final stage of the avocado's journey. They ensure that the fruit is displayed attractively and at the right ripeness to appeal to consumers. Proper handling and storage in the retail environment are essential to maintain the quality and extend the shelf life of the avocados.

## Consumption

The final stage of the avocado's lifecycle is consumption. Once purchased, avocados are enjoyed in a myriad of ways, from being sliced onto toast to being blended into smoothies or mashed into guacamole. Consumers benefit from the nutritional value and versatility of the fruit, making it a beloved addition to diets around the world.

In summary, the journey of an avocado from orchard to table is a testament to the intricate processes and dedicated efforts of those involved in its cultivation, harvesting, and distribution. Each stage is crucial in ensuring that this "green gold" reaches consumers in its best possible condition, ready to be enjoyed and celebrated for its numerous benefits.

## Key Regions for Avocado Cultivation

Avocado cultivation thrives in regions with specific climatic conditions, primarily those with mild winters and adequate rainfall. This section delves into the key regions around the world where avocados are grown, highlighting the unique characteristics and contributions of each area to the global avocado market.

## Mexico: The Heartland of Avocado Production

Mexico stands as the unrivaled leader in avocado production, contributing approximately 30% of the world's supply. The state of Michoacán, in particular, is the epicenter of this industry. The region's fertile volcanic soil, consistent rainfall, and favorable temperatures create an ideal environment for avocado trees. The state's strategic location along Mexico's Pacific coast provides access to deepwater ports, facilitating the export of avocados to international markets.

Michoacán's dominance in avocado production is also deeply rooted in its agricultural traditions.

Generations of farmers have honed their skills in cultivating this fruit, contributing to the region's reputation for producing high-quality avocados. The annual Avocado Festival in Uruapan, Michoacán, celebrates this heritage and showcases the cultural significance of avocados in the region.

## California: A Pillar of US Production

California is the leading producer of avocados in the United States, with the majority of the state's avocados coming from the coastal regions of Southern California. The Mediterranean climate, characterized by mild winters and dry summers, is perfect for avocado cultivation. The state's diverse microclimates also allow for the production of various avocado varieties, such as Hass, Fuerte, and Bacon.

California's avocado industry is well-established, with a focus on sustainable farming practices and advanced agricultural technology. The state's growers are known for their commitment to environmental stewardship, implementing water-saving irrigation techniques and integrated pest management systems. The California Avocado Commission plays a crucial role in promoting the state's avocados, ensuring they meet high standards of quality and sustainability.

## Peru: A Rising Star in Avocado Exports

In recent years, Peru has emerged as a significant player in the global avocado market. The country's diverse geography, ranging from coastal plains to the Andes mountains, provides varied climatic conditions suitable for avocado cultivation. The coastal regions, with their well-drained soils and favorable temperatures, are particularly conducive to growing Hass avocados, the most popular variety in international markets.

Peru's strategic location allows for the export of avocados to both North American and European markets, making it a key supplier during the off-season for other major producers like Mexico and California. The Peruvian government has actively supported the avocado industry through investments in infrastructure and agricultural research, further boosting the country's position in the global market.

## Chile: An Established Exporter

Chile is another prominent avocado-producing country, known for its high-quality Hass avocados. The country's unique geography, with its long coastline and varied topography, creates multiple microclimates ideal for avocado cultivation. The central regions of Chile, including Valparaíso and Coquimbo, are particularly well-suited for growing avocados due to their mild temperatures and low humidity.

Chilean avocados are primarily exported to European markets, where they are prized for their rich flavor and creamy texture. The Chilean avocado industry benefits from advanced agricultural practices and a strong export infrastructure, ensuring that the fruit reaches international markets in optimal condition. The Chilean Avocado Importers Association plays a vital role in promoting the country's avocados and maintaining quality standards.

## Other Emerging Regions

In addition to these key producers, several other countries have made notable contributions to global avocado production. Countries like Spain, Israel, and South Africa have developed robust avocado industries, leveraging their favorable climates and advanced agricultural practices. These regions primarily supply avocados to local and regional markets, contributing to the growing global demand for this versatile fruit.

In Spain, the subtropical climate of Andalusia provides ideal conditions for growing avocados, particularly the Hass variety. Israeli avocado growers benefit from the country's advanced irrigation techniques and agricultural innovation, producing high-quality fruit for both domestic consumption and export. South Africa's diverse climates allow for the cultivation of different avocado varieties, with a focus on sustainable farming practices.

The global avocado industry is supported by a diverse range of regions, each contributing unique qualities to the market. From the fertile soils of Michoacán to the innovative farming practices of California and the emerging markets of Peru and Chile, these key regions play a crucial role in meeting the ever-growing demand for avocados worldwide.

# The Role of Inspectors in Ensuring Quality

Ensuring the quality and safety of avocados as they make their way from orchards to consumers' tables is a critical aspect of the global avocado industry. Inspectors play an indispensable role in this process, safeguarding the integrity of the fruit and the trust of consumers. This section delves into the responsibilities, challenges, and significance of avocado inspectors in maintaining high standards within the industry.

## Responsibilities of Avocado Inspectors

Avocado inspectors, often employed by agencies such as the United States Department of Agriculture (USDA) and its Animal and Plant Health Inspection Service (APHIS), are tasked with a range of duties designed to ensure that only the best quality avocados reach the market. Their primary responsibilities include:

1. **Orchard Inspections:**
   - Inspectors visit avocado orchards to evaluate the health and condition of the trees and fruit. They look for signs of disease, pest infestation, and other issues that could compromise the quality of the avocados.
   - They assess farming practices to ensure they meet regulatory standards and sustainable practices.

2. **Packing Facility Inspections:**
   - At packing facilities, inspectors check the cleanliness and efficiency of operations. They ensure that avocados are handled and stored properly to prevent contamination and spoilage.
   - Inspectors verify that packing processes adhere to hygiene and safety standards, which is crucial for maintaining the quality of the avocados during transportation.

3. **Quality Control:**
   - Inspectors perform random sampling of avocados to check for size, ripeness, and overall quality. They use specific criteria to grade the fruit, ensuring only those that meet high standards are approved for export.

- They monitor the packing and labeling of avocados to ensure accuracy and compliance with international trade regulations.

**4. Pest and Disease Management:**
- One of the most critical roles of inspectors is to prevent the spread of pests and diseases that could devastate avocado crops. They check for signs of harmful pests and diseases and enforce quarantine measures when necessary.
- Inspectors implement pest management strategies and provide guidance to farmers on best practices to keep orchards pest-free.

## Challenges Faced by Inspectors

The role of avocado inspectors is not without its challenges. The complexities of international trade, environmental factors, and regional conflicts all add layers of difficulty to their work:

**1. Environmental and Climatic Challenges:**
- Inspectors must navigate varying environmental conditions that can impact avocado quality. Weather fluctuations, soil

conditions, and water availability all play roles in the health of avocado crops.
- Natural disasters, such as storms or droughts, can pose significant challenges to maintaining consistent quality.

**2. Security Risks:**
- In regions like Michoacán, where cartel influence is prevalent, inspectors face significant security risks. The threat of violence and extortion can make their work dangerous and complicated.
- Ensuring the safety of inspectors while they perform their duties is a critical concern, often requiring coordination with local authorities and additional security measures.

**3. Compliance and Regulatory Hurdles:**
- Navigating the complex web of international trade regulations and standards is a major aspect of an inspector's job. Differences in regulatory requirements between countries can complicate the inspection process.
- Keeping up-to-date with changing regulations and ensuring compliance across all levels of the supply chain is essential for maintaining market access.

# Significance of Inspection in the Avocado Industry

The role of inspectors is pivotal in upholding the standards and reputation of the avocado industry. Their work has far-reaching impacts on various stakeholders:

**1. Consumer Trust:**
- Consumers rely on the assurance that the avocados they purchase are safe, high-quality, and free from contaminants. The work of inspectors helps build and maintain this trust.
- Transparent and stringent inspection processes provide consumers with confidence in the products they buy.

**2. Market Access and Trade:**
- Quality inspections are crucial for maintaining and expanding market access. Countries importing avocados demand rigorous inspection standards to protect their own agricultural industries from pests and diseases.
- Successful inspections and adherence to regulations ensure that avocados can be exported without delays or rejections, which

is vital for the economic stability of producing regions.

## 3. Sustainability and Environmental Protection:

- Inspectors play a role in promoting sustainable farming practices by enforcing regulations that protect the environment. This includes ensuring that avocados are grown without excessive use of harmful chemicals and that orchards adhere to land use policies.
- Sustainable practices not only benefit the environment but also ensure the long-term viability of the avocado industry.

Avocado inspectors are the guardians of quality in the avocado supply chain. Their diligent work ensures that consumers receive safe, high-quality avocados while supporting the economic and environmental sustainability of the industry. Despite the challenges, their role remains crucial in maintaining the integrity and success of the global avocado market.

# Chapter 2: The Michoacán Connection

## Geographic and Agricultural Overview of Michoacán

Michoacán, a state located in the western region of Mexico, is renowned for its rich cultural heritage, diverse landscapes, and significant contributions to agriculture. Among its many agricultural products, avocados stand out as the most prominent, earning the state the title of the world's avocado capital. This section provides a comprehensive geographic and agricultural overview of Michoacán, highlighting the factors that make it an ideal region for avocado cultivation.

## Geographic Features

Michoacán is characterized by its varied topography, which includes mountains, valleys, plateaus, and coastal plains. The state covers an area of approximately 58,599 square kilometers, making it one of the larger states in Mexico. Key geographic features include:

**1. Mountain Ranges:**
- The Trans-Mexican Volcanic Belt runs through Michoacán, contributing to its diverse elevations and microclimates. This volcanic activity has played a crucial role in shaping the region's fertile soils.
- Notable peaks such as Pico de Tancítaro and Parícutin volcano are prominent landmarks.

**2. Valleys and Plains:**
- The valleys and plains of Michoacán, particularly in regions like the Bajío, provide expansive areas suitable for agriculture. These areas benefit from the accumulation of volcanic ash, which enriches the soil.

**3. Coastline:**
- Michoacán has a coastline along the Pacific Ocean, which influences the climate and weather patterns in the region. The coastal areas provide additional agricultural opportunities and access to trade routes.

## Climate and Weather

The climate in Michoacán varies significantly due to its diverse topography. However, the central and southern parts of the state, where most avocado orchards are located, generally experience a temperate climate with distinct wet and dry seasons. Key climatic features include:

**1. Temperature:**
- The average annual temperature ranges from 16°C to 22°C (60°F to 72°F), creating a favorable environment for avocado growth. The region avoids extreme temperatures, which can be detrimental to avocado trees.

**2. Rainfall:**
- Michoacán receives an average annual rainfall of 800 to 1,500 millimeters (31 to 59 inches), primarily during the summer months. This seasonal rainfall pattern is crucial for avocado cultivation, providing the necessary moisture for tree growth and fruit development.

**3. Microclimates:**
- The varied elevations and geographic features create numerous microclimates

within Michoacán. These microclimates allow for the cultivation of different avocado varieties and contribute to the overall resilience of the avocado industry in the face of climatic variability.

## Agricultural Practices

Michoacán's agricultural landscape is dominated by small to medium-sized farms, many of which are family-owned and operated. The state's agricultural sector is well-developed, with a strong emphasis on both traditional and modern farming practices. Key aspects of Michoacán's agricultural practices include:

**1. Avocado Cultivation:**
- Avocado farming in Michoacán is characterized by meticulous care and attention to detail. Farmers employ both conventional and organic farming methods, with a growing trend towards sustainable practices to protect the environment and ensure long-term productivity.
- The use of advanced agricultural technologies, such as drip irrigation systems, pest management strategies, and soil health

monitoring, enhances the efficiency and yield of avocado orchards.

**2. Diverse Crops:**
- While avocados are the most significant crop, Michoacán's agricultural sector is diverse. The state also produces significant quantities of lemons, berries, and various vegetables. This diversification helps stabilize the agricultural economy and provides multiple sources of income for farmers.

**3. Cooperative Systems:**
- Many avocado farmers in Michoacán are part of cooperatives, which provide support in terms of resources, knowledge sharing, and market access. These cooperatives play a crucial role in ensuring that small-scale farmers can compete in both national and international markets.

## Economic Impact

The avocado industry in Michoacán is a major economic driver, providing livelihoods for thousands of families and contributing significantly to the state's GDP. Key economic aspects include:

## 1. Employment:
- Avocado farming and related industries, such as packaging and transportation, create substantial employment opportunities. This industry supports jobs not only in rural areas but also in urban centers where processing and export activities are concentrated.

## 2. Export Revenue:
- Avocados from Michoacán are exported worldwide, with the United States being the largest market. The revenue generated from avocado exports is a vital source of income for the state, fueling further investment in agricultural infrastructure and community development.

## 3. Infrastructure Development:
- The success of the avocado industry has spurred investments in infrastructure, including roads, irrigation systems, and storage facilities. These improvements benefit the broader agricultural sector and enhance the overall quality of life for residents.

In conclusion, Michoacán's geographic and agricultural features create an ideal environment for avocado cultivation. The combination of fertile volcanic soils, a temperate climate, and advanced farming practices ensures that Michoacán remains at the forefront of the global avocado industry. The economic impact of avocado farming extends beyond individual farmers, contributing to the prosperity and development of the entire region.

## The Soil and Climate: Why Michoacán is Ideal for Avocados

Michoacán, a state in western Mexico, stands out as one of the world's premier regions for avocado cultivation. Its unique combination of soil, climate, and geographic features creates an ideal environment for growing high-quality avocados. This section explores the specific factors that make Michoacán a perfect haven for avocado farming.

## Geographic and Climatic Conditions

Michoacán's geography and climate play a critical role in its suitability for avocado cultivation. The state is located along Mexico's Pacific coast and features a volcanic belt that provides a fertile landscape for agriculture.

1. **Elevation and Topography:**
    - Michoacán's varied elevation, ranging from sea level to over 2,000 meters above sea level, allows for diverse microclimates. This variation is beneficial for different stages of avocado growth and helps in extending the harvesting season.
    - The state's rugged terrain and volcanic soils are particularly advantageous for avocado trees, which thrive in well-drained soils that prevent root rot and other moisture-related issues.

2. **Climate:**
    - The climate in Michoacán is classified as temperate with a distinct wet and dry season. This climate is ideal for avocados, which require a balance of moisture and dry periods for optimal growth.
    - The average annual temperature ranges from 16°C to 24°C (60°F to 75°F), providing a stable growing environment that avoids the

extremes of heat and cold that can damage the fruit.

3. **Rainfall:**
   - Michoacán receives an average annual rainfall of 1,000 to 1,500 millimeters (39 to 59 inches), predominantly during the summer months. This rainfall is critical during the early stages of avocado fruit development.
   - The dry season, which typically spans from November to April, coincides with the harvest period, reducing the risk of disease and spoilage that can occur with excessive moisture.

## Soil Composition

The volcanic origin of Michoacán's soil is a key factor in its agricultural productivity. Avocado trees benefit significantly from the mineral-rich, well-drained soils found in this region.

1. **Volcanic Soils:**
   - The soil in Michoacán is primarily andosol, a type of volcanic soil that is highly fertile and rich in minerals. These soils are known for

their excellent drainage and aeration properties, which are crucial for preventing waterlogging and promoting healthy root systems in avocado trees.
- The high organic matter content in volcanic soils supports the nutritional needs of avocado trees, fostering vigorous growth and fruit production.

**2. pH Levels:**
- Avocados prefer slightly acidic to neutral soil pH levels, ideally between 5.5 and 7.0. Michoacán's soils typically fall within this range, providing a conducive environment for avocado trees to absorb essential nutrients.
- Proper soil pH ensures the availability of key nutrients like nitrogen, phosphorus, and potassium, which are vital for the development of healthy foliage and fruit.

## Agricultural Practices

The combination of Michoacán's natural advantages with advanced agricultural practices enhances the region's avocado production.

1. **Irrigation Systems:**
   - While the region's rainfall is generally sufficient, advanced irrigation systems are employed to manage water supply during the dry season. These systems ensure that avocado trees receive adequate moisture throughout the year, optimizing fruit yield and quality.
   - Techniques such as drip irrigation are widely used to deliver water directly to the root zone, conserving water and enhancing efficiency.

2. **Sustainable Farming Practices:**
   - Many avocado growers in Michoacán adopt sustainable farming practices to preserve soil health and reduce environmental impact. These practices include crop rotation, organic fertilization, and integrated pest management.
   - Sustainable practices not only support the long-term viability of avocado orchards but also enhance the quality of the fruit by minimizing the use of chemical inputs.

Michoacán's unique combination of favorable geographic and climatic conditions, coupled with fertile volcanic soils and advanced agricultural practices, make it an ideal location for avocado cultivation. The state's natural environment provides the perfect balance of factors necessary for producing high-quality avocados, ensuring that Michoacán remains a leading player in the global avocado industry. As the demand for avocados continues to grow, the region's ability to sustainably harness these advantages will be crucial in maintaining its position as a top producer of "green gold."

## Historical Context: Growth of the Avocado Industry

The avocado industry in Michoacán has a rich history that intertwines with the region's cultural, economic, and agricultural development. This chapter explores the evolution of avocado cultivation in Michoacán, tracing its roots from ancient times to its current status as a global powerhouse in the avocado market.

## Ancient Beginnings

Avocados, native to Central and South America, have been cultivated in Mexico for thousands of years. The ancient Aztecs and other Mesoamerican civilizations were among the first to domesticate the fruit, which they called "ahuacatl." These early societies valued avocados for their rich, creamy texture and nutritional benefits, incorporating them into their diets and medicinal practices.

Archaeological evidence suggests that avocados were grown in Michoacán long before the arrival of the Spanish conquistadors in the 16th century. The region's indigenous peoples recognized the fertile volcanic soil and favorable climate as ideal conditions for cultivating avocados, establishing orchards that would lay the foundation for future agricultural practices.

## Colonial Influence and Early Trade

With the Spanish conquest came new agricultural techniques and the integration of avocados into the broader economy. Spanish settlers and missionaries spread avocado cultivation throughout the region, and the fruit began to gain recognition beyond local consumption.

During the colonial period, avocados were primarily grown for local markets, with small-scale trade emerging between different regions of Mexico. The fruit remained a staple in Mexican cuisine, appreciated for its versatility and health benefits.

## 20th Century Expansion

The true expansion of the avocado industry in Michoacán began in the early 20th century, driven by technological advancements and increasing demand. Several key developments during this period significantly boosted avocado production and trade:

**1. Improved Agricultural Practices:**
- Advances in agricultural science and techniques, including better irrigation methods, pest control, and grafting, led to higher yields and more resilient avocado trees.
- The introduction of new avocado varieties, particularly the Hass avocado, revolutionized the industry. The Hass variety, known for its superior taste, longer shelf life, and year-round production, became the dominant type grown in Michoacán.

## 2. Infrastructure Development
- Improved transportation infrastructure, including roads and railways, facilitated the movement of avocados from rural orchards to urban markets and ports. This development was crucial for expanding trade beyond local boundaries.
- The establishment of packing facilities and cold storage units helped maintain the quality of avocados during transport, reducing spoilage and extending their market reach.

## 3. Market Expansion:
- The mid-20th century saw a growing awareness and appreciation of avocados in international markets, particularly in the United States. The increasing popularity of Mexican cuisine, combined with the fruit's health benefits, drove demand.
- Michoacán's strategic location along Mexico's Pacific coast provided access to major ports, enabling the export of avocados to North America and other global markets.

## Modern Era and Global Dominance

By the late 20th and early 21st centuries, Michoacán had solidified its position as the leading avocado-producing region in the world. Several factors contributed to this dominance:

**1. Economic Incentives and Investment:**
- The Mexican government, recognizing the economic potential of avocados, implemented policies and programs to support farmers and boost production. This included subsidies, technical assistance, and investment in infrastructure.
- Private investment in avocado orchards, packing facilities, and logistics further accelerated growth, transforming the industry into a major economic driver for the region.

**2. Global Demand Surge:**
- The global demand for avocados, particularly in health-conscious markets, skyrocketed in the 21st century. Avocados became a symbol of healthy eating, featured prominently in diets, recipes, and social media.
- The popularity of avocados in the United States, Europe, and Asia created a lucrative

export market, with Michoacán supplying a significant portion of the world's avocados.

**3. Organized Production and Trade:**
- The establishment of producer associations and cooperatives helped streamline production, improve quality control, and enhance bargaining power in international markets. These organizations played a key role in promoting Michoacán avocados globally.
- Certifications and adherence to international standards ensured that Michoacán avocados met the quality and safety requirements of importing countries, further boosting their reputation.

## Challenges and Resilience

Despite its success, the avocado industry in Michoacán has faced significant challenges. Issues such as environmental concerns, water usage, and the influence of criminal organizations have posed threats to sustainable growth. However, the industry has shown resilience through:

**1. Sustainable Practices:**

- Efforts to adopt sustainable farming practices, including water conservation, reforestation, and integrated pest management, aim to mitigate environmental impact and ensure long-term viability.

**2. Security Measures:**
- Collaboration between government authorities, farmers, and industry stakeholders has led to the implementation of security measures to protect orchards and ensure the safety of workers.

**3. Technological Innovation:**
- Embracing technology, such as satellite monitoring, data analytics, and advanced farming techniques, has improved efficiency, yield, and quality control in avocado production.

The historical growth of the avocado industry in Michoacán is a testament to the region's agricultural heritage, innovation, and adaptability. From ancient cultivation to modern global dominance, Michoacán's avocados have become a symbol of excellence and a vital component of the region's economy and cultural identity. As the industry continues to evolve, balancing growth with sustainability and security will be crucial for maintaining its success and ensuring a bright future for "green gold."

# Chapter 3: The Cartel Influence

## The Entry of Cartels into the Avocado Trade

The intersection of avocados and organized crime presents a complex and troubling facet of the avocado industry, particularly in regions like Michoacán. The lucrative nature of the avocado trade, coupled with the region's socio-economic dynamics, has made it a prime target for cartel involvement. This chapter delves into how and why cartels have infiltrated the avocado industry, the methods they employ, and the impacts on local communities, farmers, and the global market.

## Origins of Cartel Involvement

The roots of cartel involvement in the avocado trade can be traced back to the broader context of organized crime in Mexico. For decades, cartels have dominated various illicit activities, including drug trafficking, extortion, and smuggling. The entry into the avocado trade represents a diversification strategy for these criminal organizations, driven by several factors:

1. **Economic Opportunity:**
   - The soaring global demand for avocados, particularly in the United States, has transformed the fruit into a highly profitable commodity. The financial allure of the "green gold" market is immense, offering cartels a substantial revenue stream beyond traditional drug trade.

2. **Strategic Geographic Advantage:**
   - Michoacán's location, with its fertile volcanic soil and favorable climate, makes it an ideal region for avocado cultivation. This same geography has historically made it a hotspot for cartel activity due to its accessibility and strategic positioning along trafficking routes.

3. **Weak Governance and Corruption:**
   - Weak governance structures, coupled with high levels of corruption, create an environment where cartels can easily exert

influence. Local authorities, often underfunded and ill-equipped, struggle to combat the pervasive power of organized crime.

## Methods of Cartel Control

Cartels employ a variety of methods to exert control over the avocado industry, ranging from intimidation and violence to sophisticated financial schemes. These methods can be broadly categorized into three main areas:

**1. Extortion and Protection Rackets:**
- Cartels often impose "protection" fees on avocado farmers, packers, and exporters. In exchange for these payments, cartels promise to protect them from other criminal elements and ensure their operations run smoothly. Failure to comply can result in threats, violence, or even death.
- This extortion racket, known locally as "derecho de piso" (right to operate), forces farmers to allocate a significant portion of their income to cartels, severely impacting their profitability and livelihood.

## 2. Control of Land and Resources:
- Cartels have been known to forcefully take over avocado orchards, either through direct seizure or by coercing landowners to sell at low prices. This land grab consolidates their control over production and increases their market share.
- In some cases, cartels engage in illegal logging and deforestation to clear land for new avocado orchards. This not only expands their agricultural footprint but also has severe environmental consequences.

## 3. Manipulation of Supply Chains:
- Cartels infiltrate various points of the avocado supply chain, from harvesting to transportation and export. By controlling these critical junctures, they can manipulate market prices, launder money, and smuggle illicit goods alongside legal shipments.
- They also bribe officials and inspectors to overlook violations or certify substandard produce, ensuring their avocados enter the market without scrutiny.

## Impact on Local Communities and Farmers

The presence of cartels in the avocado trade has profound and far-reaching impacts on local communities and farmers, exacerbating socio-economic inequalities and perpetuating a cycle of violence and fear.

**1. Economic Strain and Poverty:**
- The financial burden of paying protection fees and dealing with cartel demands significantly reduces the income of avocado farmers. Many small-scale farmers are pushed to the brink of poverty, unable to invest in their farms or improve their living conditions.
- The economic instability created by cartel activities discourages investment and development in the region, perpetuating a cycle of poverty and underdevelopment.

**2. Violence and Insecurity:**
- The pervasive threat of violence creates an atmosphere of fear and insecurity in avocado-growing regions. Farmers, workers, and their families live under constant threat,

with incidents of kidnapping, assault, and murder being disturbingly common.
- Community cohesion is often undermined as people are forced to comply with cartel demands or face retribution. The social fabric of these regions is severely damaged, leading to mistrust and fragmentation.

3. **Environmental Degradation:**
- Cartel activities, particularly illegal deforestation, have severe environmental consequences. The clearing of protected forests for avocado orchards leads to habitat destruction, loss of biodiversity, and increased greenhouse gas emissions.
- Unsustainable farming practices encouraged by cartels, such as overuse of water and chemicals, further degrade the environment and threaten the long-term viability of avocado cultivation.

## Global Market Implications

The infiltration of cartels into the avocado trade also has significant implications for the global market, affecting consumers, businesses, and regulatory bodies.

1. **Price Fluctuations and Market Stability:**
   - The manipulation of supply chains and market prices by cartels can lead to significant price fluctuations. For consumers, this means paying higher prices for avocados, while businesses face increased uncertainty and risk.
   - Market instability can deter international trade and investment, as businesses seek more stable and secure supply sources.

2. **Reputation and Ethical Concerns:**
   - The association of avocados with cartel violence and exploitation can damage the reputation of the industry. Consumers increasingly demand ethically sourced products, and the knowledge of cartel involvement can lead to boycotts and reduced demand.
   - Businesses and retailers face growing pressure to ensure their avocados are sourced from regions free from cartel influence, leading to increased scrutiny and the need for rigorous supply chain transparency.

3. **Regulatory and Policy Responses:**

- Governments and regulatory bodies must grapple with the challenge of addressing cartel influence in the avocado trade. This involves implementing and enforcing stringent regulations, enhancing law enforcement capabilities, and supporting local communities and farmers.
- International cooperation and coordinated efforts are essential to combat the transnational nature of cartel activities and ensure the integrity of the global avocado market.

## Efforts to Combat Cartel Influence

Despite the challenges, various efforts are being made to combat cartel influence in the avocado industry and protect the livelihoods of farmers and communities.

1. **Government and Law Enforcement Initiatives:**
    - The Mexican government, in collaboration with international partners, has launched operations to dismantle cartel networks and enhance security in avocado-growing regions. This includes deploying military and

police forces, improving intelligence capabilities, and targeting the financial assets of cartels.
- Strengthening the rule of law and reducing corruption are critical to these efforts, ensuring that local authorities can operate effectively and without cartel interference.

## 2. Industry and Community Responses:
- Industry associations and cooperatives are working to improve transparency and traceability in the avocado supply chain. Certification programs and standards, such as Fair Trade and organic certifications, help ensure that avocados are ethically sourced.
- Community-based initiatives, including the formation of self-defense groups known as "autodefensas," aim to protect farmers from cartel violence and reclaim control over their land and livelihoods.

## 3. International Support and Advocacy:
- International organizations and advocacy groups are raising awareness of the issue and providing support to affected communities. This includes funding for sustainable development projects, legal assistance, and

initiatives to promote human rights and environmental protection.
- Consumers and retailers play a crucial role by demanding transparency and ethical sourcing, supporting products that contribute to positive social and environmental outcomes.

The entry of cartels into the avocado trade presents a significant challenge to the integrity and sustainability of the industry. Addressing this issue requires a multi-faceted approach, involving government action, industry initiatives, community resilience, and international cooperation. By tackling the root causes of cartel influence and supporting ethical and sustainable practices, it is possible to secure a brighter future for the avocado industry and the communities that depend on it.

## Mechanisms of Control: Extortion, Corruption, and Violence

In Michoacán, the epicenter of Mexico's avocado industry, the mechanisms of control exerted by criminal organizations have profoundly influenced the region's socio-economic landscape. Extortion, corruption, and violence are integral to the operations of these groups, posing significant challenges to the avocado industry and its stakeholders.

## Extortion and Protection Rackets

Extortion is a pervasive tactic used by criminal organizations to extract payments from avocado producers and businesses operating within the industry. These extortion schemes typically involve threats of violence or other forms of coercion aimed at compelling victims to pay "protection fees" in exchange for safety or permission to conduct business without interference.

**1. Targeting Producers and Businesses:**
- Avocado growers, packing facilities, transport companies, and exporters are frequent targets of extortion. Criminal groups demand payments under the threat of violence, property damage, or disruption of operations.
- Failure to comply with these demands often results in severe consequences, including vandalism, arson, kidnapping, or even murder.

2. **Impact on Economic Viability:**
   - Extortion payments impose financial burdens on avocado producers and businesses, reducing profitability and hindering growth. The costs associated with extortion contribute to higher operational expenses and lower investment in sustainable practices.
   - Small-scale producers and businesses, lacking the resources to pay protection fees, are particularly vulnerable to exploitation, leading to economic disparity within the industry.

3. **Long-Term Consequences:**
   - The pervasive nature of extortion undermines trust and stability within the avocado supply chain. Producers may resort to clandestine operations or informal markets to avoid extortion, bypassing regulatory oversight and compromising product quality.
   - International buyers and consumers may associate Michoacán avocados with criminal activity, leading to reputational damage and potential market restrictions.

## Corruption and Complicity

Corruption among public officials and law enforcement agencies exacerbates the challenges faced by the avocado industry in Michoacán. Collusion between criminal organizations and government authorities enables illicit activities to thrive, undermining efforts to enforce regulatory compliance and uphold the rule of law.

1. **Political and Institutional Corruption:**
   - Corrupt officials, including police officers, local politicians, and regulatory inspectors, facilitate criminal activities by providing protection, information, or leniency in exchange for bribes or favors.
   - This collusion undermines efforts to combat organized crime and perpetuates a culture of impunity, where criminal actors operate with minimal risk of prosecution.

2. **Implications for Regulatory Oversight:**
   - Corrupt practices compromise the effectiveness of regulatory frameworks designed to ensure quality control and environmental sustainability in avocado production. Inspections may be

compromised or falsified, allowing substandard products to enter the market.
- The lack of accountability and transparency in regulatory processes erodes trust among industry stakeholders and undermines consumer confidence in the integrity of Michoacán avocados.

## Violence and Intimidation

Violence is a potent tool used by criminal organizations to assert dominance, eliminate rivals, and maintain control over territory and resources in Michoacán. The presence of armed groups and the use of force have profound implications for the safety and security of avocado producers, workers, and communities.

**1. Armed Conflict and Militarization:**
- Avocado-producing regions in Michoacán have experienced outbreaks of violence, including armed confrontations between rival criminal factions and clashes with security forces.
- The militarization of avocado-producing areas, with armed groups and paramilitary forces patrolling orchards and packing

facilities, creates an atmosphere of fear and insecurity.

**2. Impact on Community Welfare:**
- Violence disrupts daily life, displaces communities, and undermines social cohesion. Residents face threats of violence, forced displacement, and restrictions on movement, affecting their livelihoods and well-being.
- The psychological toll of living in a conflict zone contributes to stress, trauma, and mental health challenges among avocado producers and local residents.

**3. Human Rights Violations:**
- Human rights abuses, including extrajudicial killings, disappearances, and arbitrary detentions, are reported in areas controlled by criminal organizations. Victims often include activists, community leaders, and individuals perceived as threats to criminal interests.
- The lack of accountability for these violations perpetuates cycles of violence and impunity, creating a climate of fear and distrust in Michoacán's avocado-producing regions.

# Addressing Challenges and Building Resilience

Addressing the mechanisms of control exerted by criminal organizations requires coordinated efforts from government authorities, law enforcement agencies, industry stakeholders, and civil society. Key strategies include:

1. **Enhancing Security Measures:**
   - Strengthening law enforcement capabilities, implementing targeted security operations, and providing protection for avocado producers and businesses.
   - Promoting community policing initiatives and fostering trust between law enforcement agencies and local communities to enhance security and deter criminal activities.

2. **Combatting Corruption and Impunity:**
   - Implementing anti-corruption measures, including vetting procedures for public officials, promoting transparency in regulatory processes, and prosecuting individuals involved in corrupt practices.
   - Strengthening institutional capacity and promoting ethical standards within

government agencies to uphold the rule of law and restore public trust.

**3. Promoting Sustainable Development:**
- Supporting sustainable agricultural practices, promoting economic diversification, and investing in social programs that benefit avocado-producing communities.
- Encouraging international cooperation and partnerships to promote responsible sourcing practices and uphold human rights standards in the avocado supply chain.

Understanding and addressing the mechanisms of control—extortion, corruption, and violence—are essential for promoting stability, sustainability, and ethical practices in Michoacán's avocado industry. By tackling these challenges collectively and comprehensively, stakeholders can safeguard the industry's future, protect the well-being of communities, and uphold the reputation of Michoacán avocados in global markets.

## Case Studies of Cartel Involvement

The lucrative avocado industry in Michoacán, often referred to as "green gold," has unfortunately attracted the attention of powerful criminal organizations. These cartels have exploited the industry for financial gain, using intimidation, violence, and corruption to control various aspects of avocado production and trade. This section delves into specific case studies that highlight the extent of cartel involvement and the impact on the industry and local communities.

## Case Study 1: The Knights Templar Cartel

### Background

The Knights Templar cartel, a splinter group from La Familia Michoacana, became infamous for its brutal tactics and deep involvement in the avocado industry. Emerging in the early 2010s, the cartel exerted significant control over Michoacán's avocado orchards, exploiting farmers and establishing a reign of terror.

### Methods of Control

**1. Extortion:**

- The Knights Templar demanded "protection fees" from avocado farmers, often threatening violence or destruction of orchards if payments were not made. These fees could be a significant percentage of the farmers' income, severely impacting their profitability.
- Farmers who refused to pay faced severe consequences, including kidnapping, murder, or arson attacks on their properties.

## 2. Monopolizing Trade:
- The cartel sought to control the entire avocado supply chain, from production to distribution. They established their own packing facilities and forced farmers to sell their avocados exclusively to them, often at below-market prices.
- By controlling distribution routes and logistics, the Knights Templar could manipulate market prices and maximize their profits.

## Impact on Local Communities

The Knights Templar's involvement in the avocado industry had devastating effects on local communities:

1. **Economic Hardship:**
   - Farmers faced economic ruin due to the exorbitant extortion fees and the cartel's manipulation of market prices. Many small-scale farmers were forced out of business, losing their livelihoods and land.
   - The local economy suffered as the cartel siphoned off profits that would have otherwise contributed to community development and infrastructure.

2. **Violence and Insecurity:**
   - The pervasive violence and intimidation tactics employed by the Knights Templar created an atmosphere of fear and insecurity. Families lived in constant fear of retribution, and many were displaced as they fled the violence.
   - The presence of the cartel disrupted social cohesion and trust within communities, making collective action against the cartel difficult.

## Government Response and Aftermath

### 1. Federal Intervention:

- The Mexican government launched several military operations to dismantle the Knights Templar cartel. High-profile arrests and military presence temporarily disrupted the cartel's operations.
- Despite these efforts, the power vacuum left by the Knights Templar's decline was quickly filled by other criminal organizations, highlighting the persistent nature of cartel influence in the region.

**2. Community Vigilantes:**
- In response to the government's inability to provide adequate protection, local communities formed "autodefensa" groups—vigilante militias aimed at protecting farmers and resisting cartel control.
- These groups, although initially successful in repelling cartel influence, often became entangled in their own power struggles and allegations of human rights abuses.

## Case Study 2: The Jalisco New Generation Cartel (CJNG)

**Background**

The Jalisco New Generation Cartel (CJNG) is one of Mexico's most powerful and violent criminal organizations. Known for its aggressive expansion tactics, CJNG has increasingly turned its attention to the lucrative avocado industry in Michoacán, seeking to replicate the economic control once held by the Knights Templar.

**Methods of Control**

**1. Violent Intimidation:**
- CJNG employs extreme violence to establish dominance in the avocado industry. Their tactics include public executions, kidnappings, and threats aimed at farmers and their families.
- By demonstrating their willingness to use lethal force, CJNG instills fear and compels compliance from local farmers and business owners.

**2. Corruption and Collusion:**
- CJNG leverages corruption to secure its control over the avocado trade. They bribe local officials, police, and military personnel to turn a blind eye to their activities or actively assist them.

- This corruption undermines efforts to combat the cartel and erodes public trust in government institutions.

**Impact on the Avocado Industry**

**1. Market Disruption:**
- CJNG's involvement in the avocado industry leads to market volatility. Their control over supply chains and manipulation of prices creates uncertainty for legitimate businesses and international buyers.
- The cartel's practices, such as forcing farmers to sell at low prices or diverting shipments, disrupt the consistent supply of avocados, impacting the global market.

**2. Human Rights Violations:**
- The human cost of CJNG's control is immense. Farmers and their families suffer from extortion, violence, and displacement. Many live in fear of reprisal if they speak out or attempt to resist the cartel's demands.
- The cartel's presence exacerbates existing social and economic inequalities, leaving communities vulnerable and disenfranchised.

**Government Response and Challenges**

**1. Law Enforcement Efforts:**
- The Mexican government, in collaboration with international partners, has intensified efforts to combat CJNG. High-profile arrests and targeted operations aim to dismantle the cartel's leadership and operational capacity.
- Despite these efforts, CJNG's decentralized structure and ability to regenerate leadership complicate efforts to eradicate their influence.

**2. International Cooperation:**
- Recognizing the transnational nature of CJNG's operations, international cooperation has become crucial. The United States and other countries have provided support through intelligence sharing, training, and financial sanctions against cartel leaders.
- Cross-border efforts aim to disrupt the cartel's supply chains and financial networks, reducing their capacity to operate effectively.

# Case Study 3: Local Cartel Influence and Community Resistance

## Background

In addition to major cartels like the Knights Templar and CJNG, numerous local criminal organizations have emerged to exploit the avocado industry in Michoacán. These smaller groups often operate with similar tactics but on a more localized scale.

## Methods of Control

### 1. Protection Rackets:
- Local cartels establish protection rackets, demanding regular payments from farmers in exchange for "protection" from other criminal elements. These payments are often enforced through violence or threats.
- The proliferation of multiple groups leads to overlapping demands and increased financial burdens on farmers.

### 2. Control of Distribution Networks:
- Local cartels often seek to control regional distribution networks, ensuring that

avocados pass through their hands before reaching national or international markets.
- They impose taxes on transporters and packing facilities, further squeezing the profit margins of legitimate businesses.

**Impact on Local Communities**

**1. Economic Strain:**
- The financial demands of multiple cartels place immense strain on farmers and local businesses. The cost of doing business increases, and many farmers struggle to maintain profitability.
- The constant threat of violence and extortion discourages investment and stifles economic growth in affected areas.

**2. Community Response:**
- In some cases, communities have organized to resist cartel influence. Grassroots movements, supported by local leaders and civil society organizations, have sought to protect farmers and reclaim control over their livelihoods.
- These efforts, while courageous, face significant challenges, including limited

resources, internal divisions, and the persistent threat of retaliation from cartels.

## Government and International Response

### 1. Strengthening Local Governance:
- Efforts to combat local cartel influence include strengthening local governance and law enforcement. Building the capacity of municipal police and judicial systems is essential for providing sustainable security.
- Community policing initiatives and partnerships with civil society aim to restore trust and empower local residents to resist criminal control.

### 2. International Support:
- International organizations and foreign governments have provided support through funding, training, and capacity-building programs. These initiatives focus on enhancing the resilience of local communities and supporting sustainable agricultural practices.
- Trade policies and certification programs also aim to ensure that avocados entering international markets are produced ethically and free from cartel influence.

In conclusion, the involvement of cartels in Michoacán's avocado industry presents a complex and multifaceted challenge. Through case studies of the Knights Templar, CJNG, and local criminal organizations, it becomes evident that cartel influence extends beyond simple extortion, deeply affecting the economic, social, and security landscape of the region. Addressing this issue requires a coordinated effort that includes law enforcement, government policy, community resilience, and international cooperation. Only through comprehensive and sustained action can the avocado industry in Michoacán thrive free from the shadow of cartel control.

# Chapter 4: The Crisis

## The Incident: Assault and Detention of US Inspectors

The avocado industry in Michoacán faced a significant crisis in mid-2024, highlighting the precarious intersection of agriculture and organized crime in the region. This chapter details the incident involving the assault and detention of two US inspectors, the ensuing international ramifications, and the broader implications for the avocado trade.

## Background of the Incident

In June 2024, two US Department of Agriculture (USDA) inspectors were conducting routine inspections in Michoacán, ensuring that avocados destined for the US market met quality and phytosanitary standards. These inspections are a critical part of the trade agreement between the US and Mexico, aimed at preventing pests and diseases from crossing borders.

While traveling between orchards, the inspectors encountered a police roadblock on a highway. The roadblock, ostensibly set up by local police officers protesting pay issues, was a common sight in the region, where law enforcement and public service disputes occasionally spilled into public demonstrations. However, this particular incident quickly escalated beyond a simple protest.

## The Assault and Detention

As the inspectors attempted to navigate the roadblock, they were forcibly stopped and detained by police officers. Reports indicate that the officers were agitated and demanded that the inspectors present identification and explain their presence. Despite showing proper credentials, the inspectors were subjected to aggressive questioning and physical intimidation.

According to US Ambassador to Mexico Ken Salazar, the inspectors were assaulted during the encounter. Their car was seized, and they were held against their will for several hours. The situation only de-escalated after diplomatic interventions and the involvement of higher authorities, who negotiated their release.

## Immediate Repercussions

The incident triggered an immediate response from both the US and Mexican governments. The US Department of Agriculture (USDA) swiftly paused all avocado imports from Michoacán, citing safety concerns for their inspectors. This halt had an instant economic impact:

**1. Economic Losses for Mexican Growers:**
- The suspension of imports resulted in Mexican avocado growers losing tens of millions of dollars in revenue. With the US being the primary market for Michoacán avocados, the halt created a surplus of fruit that could not be exported.
- Prices for avocados in the US soared by 40% within a week, reflecting the sudden supply disruption and highlighting the dependency of the US market on Mexican avocados.

**2. Diplomatic Tensions:**

- The incident strained diplomatic relations between the US and Mexico. While Mexican officials initially downplayed the incident as nonviolent and unrelated to organized crime, the US maintained that their inspectors were assaulted and demanded a thorough investigation.
- Both countries entered into intense negotiations to address the immediate crisis and prevent future occurrences, resulting in new security guidelines for inspectors.

## Broader Implications

The assault and detention of US inspectors underscored several critical issues within the avocado industry and its intersection with organized crime:

### 1. Security Challenges:
- The incident highlighted the ongoing security challenges faced by those involved in the avocado trade in Michoacán. Inspectors, farmers, and workers all operate under the constant threat of violence and extortion from criminal organizations.

- The vulnerability of inspectors, who are pivotal to maintaining the quality and safety of the avocado supply chain, raises concerns about the sustainability of current trade practices.

## 2. Impact on Trade Relations:
- The suspension of imports had a ripple effect on trade relations between the US and Mexico. The economic interdependence of both countries in the avocado market means that any disruption has significant consequences for growers, distributors, and consumers.
- The incident prompted discussions about the robustness of existing trade agreements and the need for enhanced security measures and cooperation.

## 3. Role of Corruption:
- The involvement of local police in the detention of inspectors brought attention to the pervasive issue of corruption within law enforcement in Michoacán. Criminal organizations often exploit this corruption to exert control over various aspects of the avocado industry.

- Addressing corruption is crucial for creating a secure and stable environment for the avocado trade.

## Government and Industry Response

In the wake of the incident, both the US and Mexican governments took several steps to address the immediate crisis and improve long-term security:

### 1. New Security Protocols:
- Enhanced security protocols were established for USDA inspectors operating in Michoacán. These protocols included increased coordination with local and federal law enforcement to ensure safe passage and rapid response to any threats.
- The US also considered deploying additional security personnel to accompany inspectors during their visits to avocado orchards and packing facilities.

### 2. Diplomatic Negotiations:
- High-level diplomatic negotiations were conducted to resolve the immediate crisis and restore avocado imports. These

discussions focused on ensuring the safety of inspectors and preventing similar incidents in the future.
- The negotiations resulted in a temporary resumption of trade, contingent on the implementation of new security measures and continued dialogue between both governments.

**3. Industry Advocacy:**
- Industry groups, such as the California Avocado Commission, played a crucial role in advocating for the interests of growers and ensuring that trade disruptions were minimized. These groups worked closely with government officials to develop practical solutions and maintain market stability.
- Advocacy efforts also highlighted the need for transparency and accountability in the avocado supply chain, emphasizing the importance of ethical practices and adherence to international standards.

## Long-Term Implications

The assault and detention of US inspectors served as a wake-up call for the avocado industry, prompting a reevaluation of security, trade practices, and the role of criminal organizations. Several long-term implications emerged:

**1. Strengthening Supply Chain Security:**
- The incident underscored the need for comprehensive measures to secure the avocado supply chain. This includes addressing corruption, enhancing law enforcement capabilities, and improving coordination between stakeholders.
- Investment in technology, such as satellite monitoring and real-time tracking, can provide additional layers of security and transparency.

**2. Promoting Sustainable Practices:**
- Ensuring the sustainability of the avocado industry requires a holistic approach that addresses environmental, social, and economic factors. Sustainable farming practices, ethical trade agreements, and community engagement are essential components.
- Certification programs and international standards can help promote sustainable

practices and ensure that avocados entering global markets are produced ethically and free from criminal influence.

**3. Fostering International Cooperation:**
- The crisis highlighted the importance of international cooperation in addressing transnational challenges. Collaborative efforts between governments, industry groups, and civil society organizations are crucial for creating a secure and sustainable avocado industry.
- Ongoing dialogue and partnership can help build resilient systems that protect the interests of all stakeholders and ensure the long-term viability of the avocado trade.

The incident involving the assault and detention of US inspectors in Michoacán exposed the vulnerabilities and complexities of the avocado industry. It served as a catalyst for change, prompting governments, industry stakeholders, and communities to work together to address security challenges and promote sustainable practices. The lessons learned from this crisis will be instrumental in shaping the future of the avocado trade, ensuring that it remains a vital and ethical component of the global agricultural landscape.

# Immediate Impacts on Trade and Prices

The involvement of cartels in the avocado industry in Michoacán has profound and immediate impacts on trade and prices. These effects ripple through local, national, and international markets, creating economic volatility and affecting various stakeholders, from farmers to consumers. This section explores how cartel activities directly influence trade dynamics and market prices.

## Disruption of Supply Chains

### Supply Chain Control and Manipulation

Cartels often seek to control supply chains from production to distribution. This control allows them to manipulate the flow of avocados, creating artificial shortages or surpluses to influence prices. Their tactics include:

1. **Blocking Transportation Routes:**
   - Cartels frequently establish roadblocks or checkpoints, either demanding payment from transporters or outright seizing shipments. These actions delay or halt the movement of avocados, disrupting supply chains.
   - The unpredictability of these disruptions forces transport companies to take longer, less direct routes, increasing transportation costs and time to market.

2. **Controlling Packing Facilities:**
   - By controlling or influencing packing facilities, cartels can determine which avocados get processed and shipped. They may prioritize avocados from farmers who comply with their demands while rejecting or destroying produce from those who resist.
   - This selective processing affects the overall volume of avocados entering the market, leading to fluctuations in supply.

3. **Imposing "Taxes" on Exporters:**
   - Exporters often face additional "taxes" imposed by cartels. These fees are typically passed on to consumers, increasing the cost of avocados.

- The financial burden on exporters can lead to reduced profit margins and discourage investment in the industry.

**Impact on Quality and Consistency**

Cartel control also affects the quality and consistency of avocados reaching the market:

**1. Reduced Quality Control:**
- Under cartel influence, quality control measures may be compromised. Cartels prioritize speed and volume over quality, leading to inferior avocados entering the market.
- Substandard produce can damage the reputation of Michoacán avocados, reducing demand and prices in the long term.

**2. Inconsistent Supply:**
- The disruptions caused by cartels lead to inconsistent supply levels. Consumers and retailers face uncertainty regarding the availability of avocados, making it difficult to plan purchases and pricing strategies.
- This inconsistency is particularly problematic for large retailers and food

service providers, who rely on steady supplies to meet customer demand.

## Price Volatility

**Short-Term Price Spikes**

The immediate impact of cartel activities on prices is often seen in short-term price spikes. Several factors contribute to these sudden increases:

**1. Supply Shortages:**
- When cartels disrupt supply chains, the reduced availability of avocados in the market leads to higher prices. Consumers compete for limited supplies, driving up prices rapidly.
- For example, when the U.S. suspended avocado imports from Michoacán in response to the assault on inspectors, prices soared by 40% within a week.

**2. Increased Transportation Costs:**
- The additional costs incurred by transporters due to cartel-imposed roadblocks and longer routes are passed on to consumers. These

increased costs are reflected in higher retail prices for avocados.
- Exporters facing cartel "taxes" also raise prices to offset these expenses, further contributing to price increases.

**Long-Term Price Instability**

While short-term price spikes are immediate and noticeable, the long-term impacts of cartel involvement create ongoing price instability:

**1. Market Uncertainty:**
- The constant threat of cartel disruptions introduces significant uncertainty into the market. Buyers and sellers alike face difficulties in predicting future prices and supply levels.
- This uncertainty discourages investment in the avocado industry, as stakeholders are wary of potential losses due to market volatility.

**2. Erosion of Consumer Trust:**
- Frequent price fluctuations and inconsistent supply erode consumer trust. Retailers and consumers may seek more stable

alternatives, reducing demand for avocados from Michoacán.
- The loss of consumer trust can have lasting effects on the industry, as rebuilding reputation and market share is challenging.

**3. Impact on Contracts and Agreements:**
- Long-term contracts and agreements between producers, exporters, and retailers become difficult to maintain. The inability to guarantee consistent supply and pricing leads to the breakdown of these arrangements.
- This breakdown further destabilizes the market, as stakeholders must constantly renegotiate terms and conditions based on the latest disruptions.

## Economic Impact on Farmers and Local Communities

### Financial Strain on Farmers

Cartel involvement places significant financial strain on avocado farmers:

1. **Increased Costs:**
   - Farmers face increased costs due to cartel demands for protection payments and taxes. These expenses reduce their profit margins and financial stability.
   - The need to comply with cartel demands often forces farmers to cut corners in other areas, such as quality control and sustainability practices.

2. **Reduced Income:**
   - With cartels controlling market prices and dictating terms, farmers often receive lower payments for their produce. This reduction in income makes it difficult to cover operating costs and invest in future production.
   - Farmers who resist cartel demands face the risk of losing their entire harvest, either through cartel retaliation or exclusion from controlled packing facilities.

**Community Impact**

The broader community also suffers from the economic instability caused by cartels:

1. **Reduced Economic Activity:**
   - The economic uncertainty and reduced profitability of the avocado industry lead to decreased economic activity in local communities. Businesses dependent on the industry, such as suppliers and service providers, experience reduced demand.
   - Lower incomes for farmers and workers translate into reduced spending power, affecting local businesses and services.

2. **Social Disruption:**
   - The presence of cartels and the associated violence and corruption create social disruption. Families face displacement, and community cohesion is weakened as trust in authorities and institutions erodes.
   - The psychological impact of living under constant threat and economic uncertainty takes a toll on community well-being and resilience.

# International Trade Implications

### Trade Relations and Policies

Cartel involvement in the avocado industry has significant implications for international trade relations and policies:

**1. Strained Bilateral Relations:**
- Incidents such as the assault on U.S. inspectors strain trade relations between Mexico and major importers like the United States. These tensions can lead to temporary suspensions of trade and the imposition of stricter regulations.
- Diplomatic efforts to resolve these issues require time and resources, during which trade may be disrupted.

**2. Increased Regulatory Scrutiny:**
- Importing countries may impose stricter regulatory scrutiny on avocados from regions with known cartel activity. This includes more rigorous inspections, certification requirements, and compliance with sustainability standards.
- While these measures aim to ensure the quality and legality of imports, they also increase the cost and complexity of exporting avocados.

**Market Diversification**

To mitigate the risks associated with cartel involvement, stakeholders may seek to diversify their supply sources:

**1. Investment in Alternative Regions:**
- Importers and retailers may invest in avocado production in other regions or countries, reducing their reliance on Michoacán. This diversification spreads the risk and stabilizes supply chains.
- Alternative regions with stable governance and lower levels of criminal activity become more attractive to investors and buyers.

**2. Development of Domestic Production:**
- Some countries, such as the United States, may increase their domestic avocado production to reduce dependence on imports. This involves investing in agricultural research, expanding suitable growing areas, and supporting local farmers.
- While domestic production can provide a buffer against international disruptions, it may not fully replace the volume and quality of avocados from established producing regions like Michoacán.

The immediate impacts of cartel involvement in the avocado industry are far-reaching and multifaceted. Supply chain disruptions, price volatility, economic strain on farmers, and international trade implications all contribute to a complex and challenging environment. Addressing these issues requires coordinated efforts at multiple levels, including enhanced security measures, improved governance, support for local communities, and strategic market diversification. Only through comprehensive and sustained action can the avocado industry in Michoacán achieve stability and continue to thrive in the global market.

## Diplomatic and Economic Repercussions

The involvement of criminal organizations in Michoacán's avocado industry has far-reaching diplomatic and economic repercussions, affecting trade relations, market stability, and international cooperation. This section examines these consequences in detail, exploring how cartel activities impact the broader economic landscape and the diplomatic efforts to address these challenges.

## Economic Repercussions

### Market Instability and Price Volatility

The infiltration of cartels into the avocado industry creates significant market instability. Cartel activities such as extortion, violence, and manipulation of supply chains disrupt the regular flow of avocados from orchards to markets. These disruptions can lead to:

**1. Supply Shortages:**
- Violence and intimidation can force farmers to abandon their orchards or limit production, reducing the overall supply of avocados. This scarcity can lead to supply shortages in both domestic and international markets.
- Cartels' control over distribution networks can further exacerbate supply issues, as they may divert shipments or hoard avocados to manipulate market prices.

## 2. Price Volatility:
- The uncertainty created by cartel activities often results in significant price volatility. For example, the US avocado import suspension in response to the assault on inspectors led to a temporary 40% price spike .
- Price volatility affects not only consumers but also businesses throughout the supply chain, from exporters to retailers, complicating financial planning and investment decisions.

## Economic Losses and Increased Costs

### 1. Direct Economic Losses:
- Farmers and producers bear the brunt of economic losses due to extortion payments, destruction of crops, and the costs associated with cartel-imposed "taxes" on production and distribution.
- These losses reduce profitability and can drive small-scale farmers out of business, consolidating the industry under fewer, often cartel-controlled, entities.

### 2. Increased Security and Compliance Costs:

- To protect their operations, many avocado producers invest heavily in private security measures. This includes hiring armed guards, installing surveillance systems, and fortifying properties against potential attacks.
- Compliance with enhanced inspection and certification processes, implemented to ensure avocados are free from cartel influence, adds further costs. These measures, while necessary for maintaining market access, increase the overall cost of production.

**Impact on Investment and Economic Development**

**1. Deterrence of Investment:**
- The pervasive threat of violence and extortion deters both domestic and foreign investment in Michoacán's avocado industry. Investors are wary of the risks associated with operating in a region dominated by criminal organizations.
- Reduced investment hampers technological advancements, infrastructure development,

and expansion efforts, limiting the industry's growth potential.

## 2. Stagnation of Economic Development:
- The economic stranglehold exerted by cartels prevents local communities from benefiting fully from the avocado boom. Instead of reinvesting profits into community development, much of the wealth generated by the avocado industry is siphoned off by criminal organizations.
- This stagnation affects various sectors, including education, healthcare, and infrastructure, perpetuating a cycle of poverty and underdevelopment in affected regions.

# Diplomatic Repercussions

## Strained Bilateral Relations

The involvement of cartels in the avocado industry has strained diplomatic relations between Mexico and its trading partners, particularly the United States. Key issues include:

1. **Trade Suspensions and Disputes:**
   - Incidents like the temporary suspension of avocado imports by the US due to safety concerns for its inspectors underscore the fragility of trade relations. Such measures disrupt the market and highlight the challenges of ensuring safe and lawful trade.
   - Trade disputes arise when importing countries, concerned about the safety and legality of avocado shipments, impose stricter regulations or threaten embargoes. These disputes require delicate diplomatic negotiations to resolve.

2. **Pressure for Policy Reforms:**
   - International pressure, particularly from major avocado-importing countries, has prompted the Mexican government to implement policy reforms aimed at curbing cartel influence and ensuring the legality of avocado production.
   - These reforms often involve increased regulation, enhanced security measures, and stricter enforcement of anti-corruption laws, all of which require significant diplomatic coordination and support.

## International Cooperation and Support

Addressing the cartel influence in Michoacán's avocado industry necessitates extensive international cooperation. Key areas of focus include:

**1. Joint Security Initiatives:**
- Bilateral and multilateral security initiatives aim to combat the influence of cartels. These initiatives often involve intelligence sharing, joint law enforcement operations, and coordinated efforts to dismantle criminal networks.
- The US, in particular, has played a prominent role in supporting Mexico's efforts to improve security in avocado-producing regions, providing funding, training, and technological assistance.

**2. Trade Agreements and Certifications:**
- International trade agreements often include provisions to ensure that agricultural products, like avocados, are produced legally and ethically. These agreements may require certification processes to verify compliance with environmental and labor standards.

- Programs such as the US Department of Agriculture's certification of pest-free avocados involve rigorous inspection protocols that necessitate cooperation between exporting and importing countries to maintain market access.

## Diplomatic Negotiations and Advocacy

### 1. Diplomatic Negotiations:
- Diplomatic negotiations play a critical role in resolving trade disputes and ensuring the continuity of avocado trade. These negotiations often involve high-level discussions between government officials, trade representatives, and industry stakeholders.
- Issues such as inspector safety, certification processes, and measures to combat illegal land use and deforestation are central to these negotiations.

### 2. Advocacy and Public Diplomacy:
- Advocacy efforts by international organizations, non-governmental organizations (NGOs), and industry groups highlight the need for sustainable and ethical

avocado production. These efforts aim to influence policy decisions and raise awareness about the social and environmental impacts of cartel involvement.
- Public diplomacy campaigns emphasize the importance of supporting legal and sustainable avocado production, encouraging consumers to demand transparency and accountability in the supply chain.

## Broader Socioeconomic Implications

### Human Rights and Social Justice

The involvement of cartels in the avocado industry has significant human rights implications. Key issues include:

**1. Violence and Intimidation:**
- Cartel violence and intimidation tactics violate the basic human rights of farmers and their families. These actions create an environment of fear and insecurity, undermining the social fabric of communities.

- Efforts to address these human rights abuses require a comprehensive approach that includes legal protections, support for victims, and measures to hold perpetrators accountable.

**2. Labor Exploitation:**
- The use of forced labor and exploitation of workers in cartel-controlled avocado orchards raises serious ethical and legal concerns. Addressing these issues involves enforcing labor laws, providing support to exploited workers, and ensuring fair labor practices throughout the industry.

## Environmental Sustainability

**1. Deforestation and Environmental Degradation:**
- Cartel involvement in the avocado industry has led to widespread deforestation and environmental degradation. Illegal land clearing for avocado orchards contributes to habitat loss, soil erosion, and biodiversity decline.
- Efforts to promote environmental sustainability include enforcing land use

regulations, supporting reforestation projects, and encouraging sustainable farming practices.

## 2. Climate Change Impacts:
- The environmental degradation associated with illegal avocado production exacerbates climate change impacts, affecting local and global ecosystems. Addressing these impacts requires coordinated action to promote sustainable agriculture and mitigate environmental damage.

# Economic Inequality and Development

## 1. Economic Inequality:
- The concentration of wealth and power in the hands of cartels perpetuates economic inequality in avocado-producing regions. Efforts to redistribute economic benefits and support local development are essential for addressing this inequality.
- Policies aimed at supporting small-scale farmers, providing access to resources and markets, and promoting inclusive economic growth are critical for reducing inequality.

**2. Community Development:**
- Supporting community development through infrastructure projects, education, healthcare, and social services is essential for building resilience against cartel influence. Community-based initiatives that empower local residents and promote sustainable development are crucial for long-term stability.

The involvement of cartels in Michoacán's avocado industry has profound diplomatic and economic repercussions. Addressing these challenges requires a multifaceted approach that includes diplomatic negotiations, international cooperation, and comprehensive policy reforms. By promoting sustainable and ethical avocado production, supporting local communities, and ensuring the integrity of the supply chain, it is possible to mitigate the negative impacts of cartel influence and create a more stable and prosperous future for the avocado industry.

# Chapter 5: Regulatory Framework

## Existing Bilateral Agreements and Inspection Protocols

The regulatory framework governing the avocado trade between Mexico and the United States is built upon a series of bilateral agreements and inspection protocols designed to ensure the quality, safety, and legality of avocado imports. These agreements and protocols are essential for maintaining the integrity of the supply chain and protecting the interests of producers, consumers, and both nations involved. This section delves into the existing bilateral agreements and inspection protocols, highlighting their significance, evolution, and the roles of various stakeholders.

## Bilateral Agreements

# The 1997 US-Mexico Avocado Trade Agreement

In 1997, the United States and Mexico entered into a landmark trade agreement that allowed the importation of Mexican avocados into the US market for the first time in decades. This agreement was pivotal in shaping the modern avocado trade and established the foundation for subsequent regulatory measures. Key elements of the agreement include:

## 1. Market Access:
- The agreement provided Mexican avocado producers access to the lucrative US market, significantly boosting the avocado industry in Mexico, particularly in the state of Michoacán.
- It stipulated that avocados from Mexico could be imported into the US during specific months (October through April), later expanding to year-round imports as confidence in the inspection protocols grew.

## 2. Phytosanitary Standards:
- To prevent the introduction of pests and diseases that could harm US avocado crops, the agreement established stringent

phytosanitary standards. These standards require that avocados imported from Mexico be free of pests such as the fruit fly and other quarantine-significant organisms.
- The agreement mandated the implementation of a comprehensive pest management program in Michoacán, including regular monitoring, trapping, and treatment of avocado orchards.

## The 2007 North American Free Trade Agreement (NAFTA)

The North American Free Trade Agreement (NAFTA), implemented in 1994, further solidified the trade relationship between the US and Mexico, including agricultural products like avocados. Key provisions relevant to the avocado trade include:

### 1. Tariff Reductions:
- NAFTA significantly reduced tariffs on agricultural products, facilitating the flow of goods between the US, Mexico, and Canada. This reduction in trade barriers contributed to the growth of the avocado trade and increased market access for Mexican producers.

- The agreement also eliminated non-tariff barriers that previously hindered the importation of avocados, streamlining the regulatory process.

## 2. Dispute Resolution Mechanisms:
- NAFTA established mechanisms for resolving trade disputes, providing a structured process for addressing issues related to market access, tariffs, and regulatory compliance. These mechanisms have been crucial in managing disputes arising from the avocado trade.
- The agreement encouraged greater regulatory harmonization and cooperation between the US and Mexico, fostering a collaborative approach to addressing phytosanitary concerns.

## The 2020 United States-Mexico-Canada Agreement (USMCA)

The United States-Mexico-Canada Agreement (USMCA), which replaced NAFTA in 2020, continued to support the avocado trade while introducing updates to reflect modern trade practices. Key aspects of the USMCA include:

1. **Modernization of Trade Rules:**
   - The USMCA modernized trade rules to address new challenges and opportunities in the agricultural sector. This includes provisions to enhance transparency, streamline customs procedures, and promote digital trade.
   - For the avocado industry, the agreement reinforced the commitment to science-based phytosanitary measures, ensuring that regulatory decisions are grounded in scientific evidence and risk assessment.

2. **Strengthened Labor and Environmental Standards:**
   - The USMCA introduced stronger labor and environmental standards, reflecting a commitment to sustainable and ethical trade practices. These standards aim to protect workers' rights, promote fair labor practices, and encourage environmental stewardship in agricultural production.
   - The agreement includes mechanisms for monitoring and enforcing compliance with these standards, providing a framework for addressing labor and environmental concerns in the avocado industry.

# Inspection Protocols

## USDA Animal and Plant Health Inspection Service (APHIS)

The United States Department of Agriculture (USDA) Animal and Plant Health Inspection Service (APHIS) plays a critical role in ensuring the safety and quality of imported avocados. APHIS inspection protocols are designed to prevent the introduction of pests and diseases into the US while facilitating the smooth flow of trade. Key components of the APHIS inspection protocols include:

### 1. Pre-Harvest Inspections:
- APHIS inspectors conduct pre-harvest inspections in Mexican avocado orchards to ensure compliance with phytosanitary standards. These inspections involve monitoring pest populations, assessing orchard sanitation, and verifying the implementation of pest management practices.

- Inspectors work closely with Mexican agricultural authorities to conduct these inspections, fostering cooperation and ensuring adherence to international standards.

**2. Post-Harvest Inspections:**
- After harvest, avocados destined for export to the US undergo rigorous post-harvest inspections at packing facilities. APHIS inspectors examine the fruit for signs of pests, diseases, and contamination, ensuring that only pest-free avocados are certified for export.
- The inspection process includes visual inspections, laboratory testing, and verification of treatment protocols, such as cold treatment or fumigation, to eliminate any remaining pest threats.

## Mexican National Service for Agro-Alimentary Public Health, Safety, and Quality (SENASICA)

The Mexican National Service for Agro-Alimentary Public Health, Safety, and Quality (SENASICA) is responsible for regulating and overseeing the agricultural sector in Mexico, including the avocado industry. SENASICA's inspection protocols complement those of APHIS and ensure that Mexican avocados meet international standards. Key elements of SENASICA's inspection protocols include:

1. **Orchard Certification:**
   - SENASICA certifies avocado orchards that meet phytosanitary standards and comply with pest management practices. This certification is a prerequisite for exporting avocados to the US and other markets.
   - The certification process involves regular inspections, pest monitoring, and adherence to best agricultural practices to minimize the risk of pest infestations.

2. **Traceability and Record-Keeping:**
   - SENASICA requires avocado producers and exporters to maintain detailed records of their production, pest management, and treatment practices. These records are essential for traceability and help ensure the integrity of the supply chain.
   - Inspectors verify these records during inspections, cross-referencing them with physical inspections and laboratory test

results to confirm compliance with phytosanitary standards.

## Evolution and Challenges of Inspection Protocols

### Evolution of Inspection Protocols

Inspection protocols for avocados have evolved over time to address emerging challenges and incorporate advancements in technology and pest management. Key developments in the evolution of inspection protocols include:

**1. Increased Collaboration:**
- Enhanced collaboration between APHIS and SENASICA has led to more coordinated and effective inspection processes. Joint training programs, information sharing, and regular meetings have strengthened the partnership between US and Mexican regulatory authorities.
- Bilateral agreements have facilitated this collaboration, providing a framework for joint inspections, mutual recognition of

certification standards, and harmonization of regulatory practices.

## 2. Adoption of Advanced Technologies:
- The use of advanced technologies, such as remote sensing, geographic information systems (GIS), and molecular diagnostics, has improved the efficiency and accuracy of pest detection and monitoring. These technologies enable inspectors to identify pest hotspots, track pest movements, and respond more quickly to emerging threats.
- Innovations in treatment technologies, such as ozone treatment and integrated pest management (IPM) strategies, have also enhanced the effectiveness of pest control measures while minimizing environmental impacts.

**Challenges in Inspection Protocols**

Despite significant progress, inspection protocols for avocados face several challenges that require ongoing attention and adaptation. Key challenges include:

**1. Dealing with Cartel Influence:**

- The pervasive influence of cartels in the avocado industry poses significant challenges for inspectors. Intimidation, violence, and corruption can compromise the integrity of inspection processes and hinder efforts to ensure compliance with phytosanitary standards.
- Addressing this challenge requires robust security measures, anti-corruption initiatives, and support for inspectors working in high-risk areas.

## 2. Ensuring Consistency and Compliance:
- Ensuring consistent application of inspection protocols across diverse production regions and facilities is a complex task. Variability in local practices, resource availability, and enforcement capabilities can lead to inconsistencies in compliance with phytosanitary standards.
- Standardized training programs, rigorous auditing processes, and capacity-building initiatives are essential for maintaining consistency and ensuring that all stakeholders adhere to established protocols.

## 3. Adapting to Emerging Pest Threats:

- The emergence of new pest threats, driven by factors such as climate change and global trade, requires continuous adaptation of inspection protocols. Proactive surveillance, research, and innovation in pest management strategies are critical for staying ahead of these threats.
- Collaborative efforts between research institutions, regulatory authorities, and industry stakeholders are necessary to develop and implement effective responses to emerging pest challenges.

The regulatory framework governing the avocado trade between Mexico and the United States is built upon a foundation of bilateral agreements and rigorous inspection protocols designed to ensure the quality, safety, and legality of avocado imports. These measures are essential for maintaining market stability, protecting agricultural interests, and promoting sustainable and ethical trade practices.

The evolution of these agreements and protocols reflects the ongoing efforts to address emerging challenges, incorporate technological advancements, and enhance collaboration between regulatory authorities. However, significant challenges remain, including the pervasive influence of cartels, the need for consistency in compliance, and the adaptation to emerging pest threats.

By continuing to strengthen and refine these regulatory measures, the US and Mexico can ensure the long-term sustainability and integrity of the avocado industry, benefiting producers, consumers, and the broader agricultural sector.

## The Role of the USDA and APHIS in Avocado Trade

The United States Department of Agriculture (USDA) and its Animal and Plant Health Inspection Service (APHIS) play crucial roles in regulating and facilitating the trade of avocados between Mexico and the United States. Their responsibilities encompass ensuring the safety, quality, and legality of avocado imports, protecting domestic agriculture, and supporting international trade relations. This section delves into the specific functions and impact of the USDA and APHIS in the avocado trade.

## USDA and APHIS: An Overview

The USDA is a federal department responsible for overseeing agriculture, forestry, and food. It aims to meet the needs of farmers and ranchers, promote agricultural trade and production, ensure food safety, protect natural resources, and foster rural communities.

APHIS, a division within the USDA, focuses on protecting the health and value of American agriculture and natural resources. Its activities include safeguarding animal and plant health, regulating genetically engineered organisms, administering the Animal Welfare Act, and carrying out wildlife damage management activities.

In the context of the avocado trade, APHIS is particularly involved in regulating the importation of plant products to prevent the introduction and spread of pests and diseases that could harm US agriculture.

## Ensuring Pest-Free Imports

One of the primary concerns of the USDA and APHIS is preventing the introduction of pests and diseases that could devastate domestic crops. For avocados, this involves a rigorous inspection process to ensure that imported fruit is free from harmful pests such as the avocado seed weevil and the avocado stem weevil.

**1. Inspection and Certification Process:**
- APHIS inspectors in Mexico conduct detailed examinations of avocado orchards and packing facilities to ensure compliance with US phytosanitary standards. This process includes checking for signs of pest infestations and verifying that appropriate pest control measures are in place.
- Before avocados can be shipped to the US, they must be certified by APHIS as meeting all necessary health and safety standards. This certification process is crucial for maintaining the integrity of the US avocado market and protecting domestic agriculture.

**2. On-Site Inspections:**
- APHIS maintains a presence in Michoacán, Mexico, where the majority of US-bound avocados are grown. Inspectors are stationed at packing facilities and orchards to conduct on-site inspections, ensuring that avocados meet US import requirements.

- These inspectors are responsible for identifying any potential pest risks and verifying that the avocados are processed in a manner that mitigates these risks. Their presence is vital for maintaining a high standard of safety and quality in imported avocados.

3. **Risk Management and Mitigation:**
   - APHIS employs a risk-based approach to pest management, identifying and prioritizing the most significant threats to US agriculture. This involves ongoing monitoring and assessment of pest risks associated with imported avocados.
   - The agency works closely with Mexican agricultural authorities to implement effective pest control measures and ensure that these measures are consistently applied across the supply chain.

## Promoting Safe and Legal Trade

The USDA and APHIS are also involved in ensuring that avocado trade is conducted legally and ethically, addressing issues such as illegal land use, environmental sustainability, and labor practices.

1. **Enforcement of Legal Standards:**
   - APHIS inspectors are tasked with ensuring that avocados imported into the US are produced in compliance with legal standards, including those related to land use and environmental protection. This involves verifying that avocados are not grown on illegally cleared land and that sustainable farming practices are employed.
   - The agency collaborates with Mexican authorities to enforce these standards and take corrective action when violations are identified. This collaboration is essential for maintaining the integrity of the avocado supply chain and protecting the environment.

2. **Support for Sustainable Practices:**
   - The USDA promotes sustainable agricultural practices through various programs and initiatives, providing technical assistance and support to avocado producers in Mexico. This includes guidance on best practices for pest management, soil conservation, and water use.
   - By supporting sustainable practices, the USDA helps ensure that avocado production

is environmentally responsible and socially equitable, benefiting both producers and consumers.

### 3. Combating Illegal Activities:
- APHIS and the USDA work to combat illegal activities associated with avocado production, such as the involvement of criminal organizations and the exploitation of labor. This involves close coordination with law enforcement agencies and other stakeholders to identify and address illegal practices.
- Efforts to combat illegal activities include increased inspections, stricter enforcement of regulations, and initiatives to raise awareness about the importance of ethical and legal production practices.

## Facilitating International Trade

The USDA and APHIS play a pivotal role in facilitating the smooth flow of avocado trade between Mexico and the US, addressing trade barriers, and fostering cooperation between the two countries.

1. **Negotiation and Implementation of Trade Agreements:**
   - The USDA is involved in negotiating and implementing trade agreements that govern the import and export of agricultural products, including avocados. These agreements establish the rules and standards for trade, ensuring that both countries benefit from fair and transparent trade practices.
   - APHIS works to ensure that the phytosanitary measures outlined in these agreements are effectively implemented, reducing the risk of pest and disease introduction while facilitating the movement of avocados across borders.

2. **Diplomatic Coordination:**
   - The USDA and APHIS engage in diplomatic coordination with Mexican authorities to address issues related to avocado trade. This includes regular communication, joint inspections, and collaborative efforts to resolve trade disputes and ensure compliance with trade agreements.
   - Diplomatic coordination is essential for maintaining a stable and reliable avocado supply chain, addressing challenges such as

pest outbreaks, trade suspensions, and market fluctuations.

3. **Technical Assistance and Capacity Building:**
   - The USDA provides technical assistance and capacity-building support to Mexican agricultural authorities and avocado producers. This includes training programs, workshops, and the provision of resources to enhance the effectiveness of pest management and inspection processes.
   - By building capacity in Mexico, the USDA helps ensure that avocados exported to the US meet the highest standards of quality and safety, benefiting both countries.

## Addressing Challenges and Future Directions

The USDA and APHIS face ongoing challenges in regulating the avocado trade, including the need to adapt to evolving pest threats, address illegal activities, and respond to market dynamics. Future directions for these agencies involve:

1. **Enhancing Inspection and Certification Processes:**
   - Continuous improvement of inspection and certification processes is essential for maintaining the safety and quality of imported avocados. This includes adopting new technologies, refining risk assessment methods, and ensuring that inspectors are well-trained and equipped to carry out their duties.
   - Innovations such as remote sensing, data analytics, and automated inspection systems can enhance the efficiency and effectiveness of the certification process, reducing the risk of pest introductions and improving compliance with trade standards.

2. **Strengthening International Cooperation:**
   - Strengthening international cooperation is critical for addressing the complex challenges associated with the avocado trade. This includes fostering closer collaboration with Mexican authorities, industry stakeholders, and international organizations to promote sustainable and ethical production practices.
   - Enhanced cooperation can lead to the development of joint initiatives, shared

resources, and coordinated efforts to combat illegal activities and support the growth of the avocado industry.

## 3. Promoting Consumer Awareness and Demand for Ethical Products:
- Educating consumers about the importance of sustainable and ethical avocado production can drive demand for legally and responsibly produced avocados. The USDA can play a role in raising awareness about the social and environmental impacts of avocado production and promoting transparency in the supply chain.
- Consumer advocacy and certification programs, such as Fair Trade and organic certifications, can help ensure that avocados are produced in a manner that benefits both producers and the environment.

## 4. Adapting to Climate Change and Environmental Challenges:
- Climate change poses significant challenges to avocado production, affecting growing conditions, pest populations, and water availability. The USDA and APHIS must adapt their strategies to address these challenges, supporting research and

- development of climate-resilient farming practices.
- Efforts to mitigate the environmental impacts of avocado production, such as reducing deforestation and promoting sustainable land use, are essential for ensuring the long-term viability of the industry.

The USDA and APHIS play a vital role in regulating and facilitating the avocado trade between Mexico and the United States. Through rigorous inspection processes, enforcement of legal standards, and international cooperation, these agencies help ensure the safety, quality, and sustainability of avocados imported into the US. By addressing ongoing challenges and promoting ethical and sustainable practices, the USDA and APHIS contribute to the stability and growth of the avocado industry, benefiting producers, consumers, and the environment.

## Proposed Changes and Their Implications

As the avocado industry grapples with the influence of cartels, various stakeholders, including governments, industry groups, and international organizations, have proposed numerous changes to address the issues. These proposed changes aim to enhance security, improve regulatory frameworks, and ensure sustainable and ethical production. This section explores these proposed changes in detail and examines their potential implications for the avocado industry, local communities, and international trade.

## Enhanced Security Measures

### Increased Protection for Inspectors

**Proposal:**
- Implement additional security measures to protect inspectors from violence and intimidation by cartels. This includes the use of armed escorts, secure transportation, and fortified inspection facilities.

**Implications:**
**1. Safety and Efficiency:**
- Enhanced security measures would ensure the safety of inspectors, allowing them to perform their duties without fear of violence.

This would improve the efficiency and reliability of the inspection process.

**2. Cost Considerations:**
- The implementation of these measures would incur significant costs, which may be passed on to producers and, ultimately, consumers. However, the benefits of a secure and stable supply chain could outweigh these costs.

**3. Collaboration and Trust:**
- Strengthening security measures would require close collaboration between Mexican and US authorities, fostering trust and cooperation. This could lead to more effective joint efforts in combating cartel influence.

### Increased Presence of Law Enforcement

**Proposal:**
- Increase the presence of federal law enforcement in key avocado-producing regions to deter cartel activities and provide a safer environment for farmers and workers.

**Implications:**

1. **Deterrence of Criminal Activities:**
   - A heightened law enforcement presence would deter criminal activities, reducing extortion, violence, and illegal land use. This would create a more stable and secure environment for avocado production.
2. **Community Relations:**
   - Effective law enforcement requires building positive relationships with local communities. This involves ensuring that law enforcement actions are respectful of human rights and do not exacerbate existing tensions.
3. **Resource Allocation:**
   - Increasing law enforcement presence necessitates significant resource allocation, including funding, personnel, and training. Balancing these resources with other priorities could be challenging.

# Regulatory and Certification Reforms

## Strengthening Certification Processes

**Proposal:**

- Enhance the certification processes to ensure that avocados are produced legally and ethically, free from cartel influence. This includes stricter oversight of land use, environmental impact, and labor practices.

**Implications:**
**1. Market Access and Consumer Confidence:**
- Strengthened certification processes would improve market access by ensuring that avocados meet international standards. This would enhance consumer confidence in the integrity and quality of the products.

**2. Compliance Costs:**
- Producers would need to invest in compliance measures, including documentation, audits, and potentially changing farming practices. These costs could be significant, especially for small-scale farmers.

**3. Sustainable Practices:**
- Emphasizing sustainable and ethical production practices would have long-term benefits for the environment and local communities. This includes reducing deforestation, protecting biodiversity, and ensuring fair labor conditions.

## Implementing Traceability Systems

### Proposal:
- Develop and implement traceability systems that track avocados from farm to table. This includes using technology such as blockchain to provide transparency and accountability throughout the supply chain.

### Implications:
#### 1. Transparency and Accountability:
- Traceability systems would increase transparency and accountability, making it easier to identify and address issues related to illegal activities and unethical practices.

#### 2. Technological Challenges:
- Implementing traceability systems requires significant technological infrastructure and expertise. Small-scale farmers and producers in remote areas may face challenges in adopting these technologies.

#### 3. Consumer Engagement:
- Providing consumers with information about the origin and production of avocados could enhance their engagement and willingness to pay a premium for ethically produced products.

# Environmental and Land Use Policies

### Enforcing Land Use Regulations

**Proposal:**
- Enforce stricter land use regulations to prevent illegal deforestation and ensure that avocado orchards are established and maintained in compliance with environmental laws.

**Implications:**
**1. Environmental Protection:**
- Enforcing land use regulations would protect forests, biodiversity, and ecosystems. This would contribute to the long-term sustainability of the avocado industry and mitigate climate change impacts.

**2. Economic Displacement:**
- Strict enforcement may lead to the displacement of farmers who have established orchards on illegally cleared land. Providing support and alternative livelihoods for these farmers is essential to avoid economic hardship.

**3. Collaboration with Environmental Organizations:**

- Collaborating with environmental organizations and experts would enhance the effectiveness of land use policies and promote best practices in sustainable agriculture.

## Promoting Reforestation and Conservation

**Proposal:**
- Implement reforestation and conservation programs to restore degraded lands and protect natural habitats. These programs should involve local communities and stakeholders in planning and execution.

**Implications:**
### 1. Ecosystem Restoration:
- Reforestation and conservation programs would restore ecosystems, improve soil health, and enhance water resources. This would benefit both the environment and agricultural productivity.

### 2. Community Involvement:
- Involving local communities in reforestation efforts would provide economic opportunities and foster a sense of ownership and stewardship. This would

enhance the long-term success of conservation initiatives.

3. **Funding and Support:**
   - Securing funding and support for reforestation programs is crucial. This includes government grants, international aid, and partnerships with private sector organizations committed to sustainability.

## Diplomatic and Trade Policy Adjustments

### Revising Bilateral Trade Agreements

**Proposal:**
- Revise bilateral trade agreements between Mexico and the US to include provisions that address the influence of cartels and ensure the legality and sustainability of avocado production.

**Implications:**
1. **Enhanced Cooperation:**
   - Revising trade agreements would strengthen cooperation between Mexico and the US, providing a framework for addressing

security, regulatory, and environmental issues collaboratively.

## 2. Trade Barriers and Compliance:
- New provisions may introduce trade barriers or additional compliance requirements for producers. Ensuring that these measures are fair and do not disproportionately burden small-scale farmers is essential.

## 3. Economic and Political Dynamics:
- Negotiating revisions to trade agreements involves complex economic and political dynamics. Balancing the interests of various stakeholders, including farmers, consumers, and governments, is critical for achieving mutually beneficial outcomes.

## Supporting International Advocacy and Standards

**Proposal:**
- Advocate for international standards and best practices in avocado production, including ethical labor practices, environmental sustainability, and anti-corruption measures.

**Implications:**

1. **Global Standards and Best Practices:**
   - Promoting international standards would elevate the entire avocado industry, ensuring that production practices meet high ethical and environmental criteria. This would benefit producers and consumers worldwide.
2. **Influence and Leadership:**
   - By taking a leadership role in advocating for these standards, countries like Mexico and the US can influence global policies and practices, setting a positive example for other producing and consuming nations.
3. **Challenges of Implementation:**
   - Implementing international standards across diverse regions and contexts presents challenges. Ensuring that these standards are adaptable and inclusive is crucial for their widespread adoption and effectiveness.

The proposed changes to address cartel influence in Michoacán's avocado industry are multifaceted, encompassing security measures, regulatory reforms, environmental policies, and diplomatic efforts. While each proposal presents its own set of challenges and implications, collectively, they offer a comprehensive approach to creating a more secure, sustainable, and ethical avocado industry.

By enhancing security, strengthening regulatory frameworks, promoting environmental sustainability, and fostering international cooperation, these changes aim to mitigate the negative impacts of cartel activities and ensure the long-term viability of the avocado industry. Implementing these changes requires the concerted effort of governments, industry stakeholders, and international organizations, working together to build a future where avocados can be produced and enjoyed without the shadow of cartel influence.

# Chapter 6: The Human Element

## The Lives of Avocado Farmers and Inspectors

The avocado industry, while often seen through the lens of economic figures and trade statistics, is fundamentally about people. At its core are the farmers who cultivate the "green gold" and the inspectors who ensure its quality and safety. This chapter delves into the daily lives, challenges, and aspirations of these key players, highlighting the human element that drives the avocado industry.

## The Lives of Avocado Farmers

### Daily Life on the Farm

**Routine and Responsibilities:**

- The daily life of an avocado farmer in Michoacán begins early. Farmers typically wake before dawn to manage the extensive tasks required to maintain their orchards. This includes watering, fertilizing, pruning, and monitoring the health of the trees. The work is labor-intensive and requires a deep understanding of agricultural practices and the specific needs of avocado trees.

**Economic Pressures:**
- The financial stability of avocado farmers is heavily tied to the market's fluctuations. While avocados are a lucrative crop, the costs associated with maintaining an orchard, including labor, equipment, and fertilizers, are significant. Farmers must balance these costs against the prices they can secure for their produce, which can be volatile.

**Cartel Influence:**
- Many farmers in Michoacán face the added pressure of cartel influence. Criminal organizations often demand protection payments and may exert control over land use and sales. Farmers are frequently caught between their need to protect their livelihoods and the dangers of opposing

cartel demands. This creates an environment of fear and uncertainty.

### Social and Community Impact

### Community Life:
- Avocado farming is not just an economic activity; it is deeply embedded in the social fabric of Michoacán. Farms are often family-run, with multiple generations working together. This fosters strong community ties and a collective identity centered around avocado cultivation.

### Education and Youth:
- The future of avocado farming hinges on the younger generation. However, many young people are reluctant to follow in their parents' footsteps due to the hard labor and associated risks. Education plays a crucial role in providing alternatives, but it also means that the knowledge and tradition of avocado farming could diminish over time.

### Health and Well-being:
- The physical demands of farming take a toll on the health of workers. Long hours of

manual labor can lead to chronic injuries and health issues. Additionally, the mental stress from economic pressures and threats from cartels further impacts farmers' well-being.

## Success Stories and Aspirations

### Entrepreneurial Spirit:
- Despite the challenges, many farmers demonstrate remarkable resilience and entrepreneurial spirit. Some have diversified their operations to include value-added products like avocado oil and guacamole, expanding their market reach and increasing their income.

### Innovations in Farming:
- Technological advancements are gradually being adopted by forward-thinking farmers. Innovations such as drip irrigation, disease-resistant rootstocks, and sustainable farming practices help improve yields and reduce environmental impact.

### Future Aspirations:

- Farmers aspire to a stable and secure industry where they can operate without fear and with fair economic returns. Many hope for greater support from the government and international community in terms of security, subsidies, and market access.

## The Lives of Avocado Inspectors

### Roles and Responsibilities

**Inspection Duties:**
- Inspectors are tasked with ensuring that avocados meet stringent quality and safety standards before they enter the US market. This involves visiting orchards and packing facilities to check for pests, diseases, and compliance with agricultural regulations. Their work is crucial for maintaining the trust and safety of the international avocado trade.

**Daily Challenges:**
- The role of an inspector is demanding and often dangerous. Inspectors must be meticulous and thorough in their

assessments, which requires a deep understanding of agricultural science and regulatory standards. The work involves extensive travel and long hours in the field.

**Security Risks:**
- Inspectors in Michoacán face significant security risks due to the presence of cartels. There have been incidents of threats, assaults, and even detentions by criminal groups seeking to influence the inspection process. This makes the job not only challenging but potentially life-threatening.

## Impact on Personal Life

**Family and Home Life:**
- The demanding nature of inspection work can take a toll on inspectors' personal lives. Frequent travel and long hours mean less time at home with family. The stress associated with the job can also impact personal relationships and overall well-being.

**Mental Health:**

- The constant threat of violence and the high-stakes nature of their work contribute to significant stress and anxiety. Many inspectors struggle with the psychological burden of their responsibilities and the dangers they face. Access to mental health support and counseling is crucial but often lacking.

## Professional Development and Recognition

### Training and Expertise:
- Inspectors undergo rigorous training to equip them with the skills needed to perform their duties effectively. This includes knowledge of agricultural practices, pest management, and regulatory compliance. Continuous professional development is essential to keep up with evolving standards and practices.

### Recognition and Support:
- The critical role of inspectors is often underappreciated. Greater recognition of their contributions and the risks they take is necessary. Support from both the Mexican and US governments, in terms of security

and resources, is vital for their continued effectiveness and safety.

**Career Aspirations:**
- Many inspectors aspire to advance within their field, seeking roles that offer greater responsibility and impact. Opportunities for career growth and development within regulatory agencies can help retain experienced and skilled inspectors.

The human element of the avocado industry is complex and multifaceted. Avocado farmers and inspectors are at the heart of this industry, facing unique challenges and demonstrating remarkable resilience. Their daily lives, impacted by economic pressures, security risks, and the demands of their roles, paint a vivid picture of the realities behind the global avocado trade.

Understanding and addressing the needs and aspirations of these individuals is crucial for the sustainability and ethical development of the avocado industry. By recognizing their contributions and supporting their well-being, the industry can move towards a future that is not only economically viable but also just and humane.

## Personal Stories from the Field

Behind the statistics and policy discussions surrounding Michoacán's avocado industry are the personal stories of individuals whose lives are deeply intertwined with this "green gold." These stories shed light on the challenges, aspirations, and resilience of those working in the avocado fields, facing the realities of cartel influence, economic pressures, and environmental concerns.

## José's Struggle for Survival

José, a 45-year-old avocado farmer from a small village in Michoacán, has spent most of his life cultivating avocados on his family-owned orchard. For José, avocados are more than just a crop—they are his livelihood and his family's legacy. However, the presence of cartels has cast a shadow over his work.

"Every season, we live in fear," José recounts. "The cartels demand 'taxes' from us, threatening violence if we refuse. It's not just about money; it's about survival."

José describes the constant tension of navigating between paying extortion fees to armed groups and trying to protect his family and workers. The recent escalation in violence has forced him to invest in private security and rely on local community networks for protection.

"Sometimes, I wonder if it's worth it," José reflects. "But this land, these trees—they're part of who I am. I can't just walk away."

## María's Dream of Education

María, a 23-year-old agricultural worker in Michoacán, dreams of a different future. Growing up in a community dominated by avocado production, María has seen firsthand the opportunities and challenges associated with the industry.

"I want to go to university," María shares, her eyes lighting up with determination. "But it's hard. My family depends on the avocado harvest for income, and the uncertainty makes planning for the future difficult."

Despite the hardships, María remains optimistic. She volunteers with a local NGO that promotes education and sustainable farming practices, hoping to make a difference in her community.

"I believe education is the key to breaking the cycle of poverty and violence," María explains. "If we can build a stronger community, we can create a better future for everyone."

## Miguel's Fight for Environmental Justice

Miguel, a conservationist and environmental activist in Michoacán, has dedicated his life to protecting the region's natural resources from the impact of avocado production.

"The expansion of avocado orchards has led to rampant deforestation and habitat loss," Miguel laments. "Illegal land clearing for avocado cultivation not only destroys ecosystems but also threatens biodiversity and water sources."

Miguel's organization works tirelessly to document and report cases of illegal deforestation, advocating for stricter enforcement of environmental laws and sustainable land use practices.

"It's a constant battle," Miguel admits. "But seeing the impact of our work—restoring forests, protecting wildlife habitats—it keeps me going."

## Luisa's Hope for Change

Luisa, a community leader and advocate for social justice, believes in the power of collective action to bring about positive change in Michoacán.

"We cannot ignore the injustices that plague our communities," Luisa asserts. "From violence and corruption to economic inequality, we must stand together to demand accountability and transparency."

Through grassroots organizing and community empowerment initiatives, Luisa mobilizes local residents to voice their concerns and advocate for policies that prioritize human rights and sustainable development.

"We have the strength and resilience to overcome these challenges," Luisa declares. "Together, we can build a future where everyone has the opportunity to thrive."

These personal stories illustrate the human side of Michoacán's avocado industry, highlighting the courage, determination, and hope of individuals working against formidable odds. Their experiences underscore the urgent need for sustainable and ethical practices that protect both people and the environment. By amplifying these voices and supporting their efforts, we can contribute to a future where the avocado industry thrives responsibly and benefits all stakeholders involved.

## The Risks and Rewards of Working in Michoacán

Michoacán, a state nestled along Mexico's Pacific coast with fertile volcanic soil, has emerged as a global powerhouse in avocado production. However, the region's prominence in the avocado industry comes with significant risks and rewards for those involved, from farmers and laborers to industry stakeholders and international markets.

This section explores the complexities of working in Michoacán's avocado industry, highlighting the inherent risks and potential rewards associated with avocado cultivation in this dynamic region.

# Risks

**Security Threats and Violence**

**1. Cartel Influence and Criminal Activities:**
- Michoacán has earned a notorious reputation as a stronghold for drug cartels, including those deeply entrenched in the avocado trade. Cartels exert control through extortion, violence, and intimidation tactics aimed at farmers, producers, and local communities.
- Farmers and landowners often face threats to their safety and livelihoods, including demands for protection payments (known as "piso") and coercion to sell their produce at below-market rates.

**2. Violence and Intimidation:**
- Incidents of violence, including kidnappings, assassinations, and armed confrontations,

are not uncommon in Michoacán's avocado-producing regions. These acts of violence create an atmosphere of fear and uncertainty, affecting daily operations and long-term planning.

3. **Impunity and Lawlessness:**
   - Limited law enforcement presence and pervasive corruption undermine efforts to combat criminal activities effectively. The lack of accountability for perpetrators of violence and extortion further exacerbates insecurity in the region.

**Economic Vulnerability**

1. **Price Volatility and Market Instability:**
   - The dependency on avocado exports, particularly to the United States, exposes farmers and producers to fluctuations in international market prices. Disruptions in supply chains, such as export suspensions or trade disputes, can lead to sudden price hikes or market downturns.
   - Small-scale farmers, who constitute a significant portion of avocado producers in Michoacán, are particularly vulnerable to

economic shocks and may struggle to recover from financial losses.

**2. Financial Pressures and Extortion:**
- Extortion payments demanded by cartels add to production costs, reducing profit margins for farmers. Failure to comply with extortion demands can result in violence or destruction of property, compounding economic hardships.

## Environmental and Social Challenges

**1. Deforestation and Environmental Degradation:**
- The expansion of avocado cultivation has contributed to deforestation and environmental degradation in Michoacán. Illegal land clearing, often facilitated by criminal groups, threatens biodiversity, soil quality, and water resources.
- Environmental sustainability initiatives face challenges in balancing agricultural expansion with conservation efforts, raising concerns about long-term ecological impacts.

**2. Social Displacement and Inequality:**

- Land disputes and forced evictions, driven by the expansion of avocado plantations, have displaced indigenous communities and small-scale farmers from their ancestral lands. This displacement exacerbates social inequalities and disrupts traditional livelihoods.
- The concentration of wealth and economic opportunities in the hands of a few exacerbates socioeconomic disparities within the region, leading to marginalization and social unrest.

## Rewards

**Economic Opportunities and Employment**

**1. Economic Contribution:**
- The avocado industry is a major economic engine for Michoacán, generating employment opportunities and income for thousands of residents. Avocado cultivation supports a diverse workforce, including farmers, laborers, packers, and transporters.
- The industry's economic impact extends beyond agriculture, stimulating growth in

ancillary sectors such as logistics, retail, and hospitality.

## 2. Income Generation:
- Avocado farming provides a source of steady income for farmers, helping to sustain livelihoods and support household expenses. The profitability of avocado cultivation, particularly in lucrative export markets, incentivizes continued investment in the industry.

## Market Access and Global Demand

## 1. Export Market Dominance:
- Michoacán's strategic geographic location and favorable climatic conditions make it a leading global supplier of avocados, particularly to the United States. The region's reputation for producing high-quality avocados enhances its competitiveness in international markets.
- Access to export markets enables farmers and producers to capture premium prices for their products, contributing to economic growth and regional development.

2. **Global Demand:**
    - The rising global demand for avocados, driven by shifting consumer preferences towards healthy and nutritious foods, presents opportunities for market expansion and revenue growth. Michoacán's ability to meet this demand positions it as a key player in the global avocado trade.

## Technological Advancements and Innovation

### 1. Technological Integration:
- Advancements in agricultural technology, irrigation systems, and farming practices have improved productivity and efficiency in avocado cultivation. Innovations such as precision farming and automated harvesting techniques enhance yields and reduce production costs.
- Adoption of sustainable farming practices and certifications (e.g., organic farming, fair trade) underscores Michoacán's commitment to environmental stewardship and quality assurance.

## Community Development and Social Impact

### 1. Social Investment:
- Avocado industry stakeholders, including government agencies, private companies, and non-profit organizations, invest in community development initiatives. These efforts focus on education, healthcare, infrastructure, and social welfare programs.
- Community development projects aim to enhance quality of life, promote inclusive growth, and empower marginalized populations, contributing to social cohesion and resilience.

### 2. Cultural Heritage and Identity:
- Avocado farming is deeply intertwined with the cultural heritage and identity of Michoacán's indigenous communities. Traditional farming practices, knowledge sharing, and cultural celebrations reinforce local pride and cultural preservation.
- Sustainable development initiatives prioritize the preservation of cultural landscapes and indigenous knowledge systems, fostering a sense of belonging and continuity for future generations.

Working in Michoacán's avocado industry entails navigating a landscape defined by both risks and rewards. While the region offers economic opportunities, market dominance, and technological advancements, it also confronts challenges such as security threats, environmental degradation, and social inequality. Addressing these complexities requires a balanced approach that promotes sustainable development, strengthens regulatory frameworks, and fosters inclusive growth. By mitigating risks and harnessing the rewards, stakeholders can ensure a resilient and prosperous future for Michoacán's avocado industry, benefiting local communities, global markets, and environmental sustainability.

# Chapter 7: Environmental Concerns

## The Issue of Illegal Deforestation

In Michoacán, the rapid expansion of avocado cultivation has been accompanied by widespread illegal deforestation, posing significant environmental concerns and sustainability challenges. This chapter examines the issue of illegal deforestation within the context of Michoacán's avocado industry, exploring its causes, impacts, and efforts to address this critical environmental issue.

## Causes of Illegal Deforestation

**1. Demand for Agricultural Land:**
- The high demand for avocado cultivation has led to the illegal clearing of forests and natural habitats to make way for new plantations. Landowners and farmers, under pressure to meet market demands, often

engage in illegal deforestation to expand their avocado orchards.

**2. Cartel Involvement and Criminal Activity:**
 - Criminal organizations, including drug cartels, play a significant role in illegal deforestation as they seek to control land for agricultural purposes. Cartels exploit weak governance and law enforcement, using violence and intimidation to facilitate land grabs and illegal land use changes.

**3. Lack of Regulatory Enforcement:**
- Weak regulatory frameworks and enforcement mechanisms contribute to illegal deforestation. Limited oversight and corruption within local authorities enable landowners and criminal groups to operate outside the law, disregarding environmental protections and land use regulations.

# Impacts of Illegal Deforestation

**1. Loss of Biodiversity:**
- Illegal deforestation in Michoacán has resulted in the destruction of native forests and ecosystems, leading to biodiversity loss and habitat fragmentation. Endangered

species, including flora and fauna endemic to the region, are at risk of extinction due to habitat destruction.

**2. Climate Change and Carbon Emissions:**
- Deforestation contributes to increased carbon emissions and accelerates climate change. Forests act as carbon sinks, absorbing carbon dioxide from the atmosphere. Their destruction releases stored carbon, exacerbating greenhouse gas emissions and global warming.

**3. Soil Degradation and Erosion:**
- The removal of forest cover for avocado plantations exposes soils to erosion and degradation. Deforested areas are vulnerable to erosion, soil nutrient depletion, and decreased water retention capacity, affecting agricultural productivity and ecosystem resilience.

**4. Water Resource Depletion:**
- Forests play a crucial role in regulating water cycles and maintaining watershed functions. Deforestation disrupts these hydrological processes, leading to reduced water

availability, altered precipitation patterns, and increased risks of floods and droughts.

## Efforts to Address Illegal Deforestation

### 1. Legal and Regulatory Reforms:
- Strengthening land use regulations and enforcement mechanisms is essential to combat illegal deforestation. Governments and environmental agencies in Mexico are revising policies to increase penalties for illegal land clearing, enhance monitoring systems, and promote sustainable land management practices.

### 2. Forest Conservation and Restoration:
- Implementing conservation initiatives and reforestation programs is critical to restoring degraded lands and protecting remaining forests. Community-led reforestation projects engage local stakeholders in restoring ecosystems, enhancing biodiversity, and mitigating climate impacts.

### 3. International Collaboration and Support:

- Collaborating with international organizations, governments, and NGOs facilitates knowledge sharing, capacity building, and financial support for forest conservation efforts. International partnerships promote best practices in sustainable agriculture, biodiversity conservation, and climate resilience.

**4. Public Awareness and Education:**
- Raising awareness about the environmental impacts of illegal deforestation is essential to garner public support and promote responsible consumer choices. Educational campaigns emphasize the importance of forest conservation, sustainable land use practices, and ethical sourcing of agricultural products.

Illegal deforestation poses a significant threat to environmental sustainability and biodiversity conservation in Michoacán's avocado-producing regions. Addressing this complex issue requires concerted efforts from governments, industry stakeholders, and local communities to strengthen regulatory frameworks, promote sustainable land management practices, and foster international cooperation. By combating illegal deforestation, protecting forest ecosystems, and restoring degraded lands, stakeholders can safeguard the ecological integrity of Michoacán while ensuring the long-term viability of the avocado industry.

## Environmental Impact of Avocado Farming

Avocado farming, particularly in regions like Michoacán, Mexico, where it is a major industry, has significant environmental impacts that affect ecosystems, biodiversity, water resources, and climate stability. While avocado cultivation offers economic benefits, the environmental consequences must be carefully managed to ensure sustainable practices and mitigate long-term damage. This section explores the environmental impact of avocado farming, highlighting key issues and potential solutions to promote environmental stewardship in the industry.

## Deforestation and Habitat Loss

**1. Expansion of Agricultural Land:**

- The demand for avocado production has driven the conversion of natural ecosystems, including forests and grasslands, into agricultural land. In Michoacán, this expansion often involves clearing native forests to establish avocado orchards, leading to habitat loss for wildlife species and disruption of ecological balance.
- Deforestation not only reduces biodiversity but also diminishes carbon storage capacity, contributing to greenhouse gas emissions and exacerbating climate change.

## 2. Impact on Biodiversity:
- Deforestation fragments habitats and isolates wildlife populations, increasing their vulnerability to extinction. Loss of habitat for endemic species, including plants, animals, and insects, threatens biodiversity hotspots and undermines ecosystem resilience.
- Avocado monoculture, characterized by the cultivation of a single crop over extensive areas, reduces landscape diversity and limits opportunities for species to thrive in diverse habitats.

## Water Resource Management

### 1. Water Consumption:
- Avocado trees are water-intensive crops, requiring significant amounts of irrigation to support growth and fruit development. In regions with limited water resources, such as Michoacán, intensive irrigation practices can lead to water stress, depletion of aquifers, and competition for water among agricultural, urban, and environmental needs.
- Unsustainable water extraction practices jeopardize local water supplies, affecting communities, ecosystems, and agricultural productivity.

### 2. Impact on Water Quality:
- Agrochemical inputs, including fertilizers and pesticides used in avocado farming, can leach into water bodies, contaminating groundwater and surface water sources. Chemical runoff from orchards poses risks to aquatic ecosystems, compromising water quality and biodiversity.
- Efforts to minimize agricultural runoff and adopt eco-friendly farming practices are

critical to safeguarding water resources and preserving ecosystem health.

## Soil Health and Erosion Control

### 1. Soil Degradation:
- Intensive farming practices, such as monoculture and heavy machinery use, contribute to soil erosion, compaction, and nutrient depletion. Avocado orchards, especially on steep slopes or vulnerable soils, are susceptible to erosion, which undermines soil fertility and productivity over time.
- Sustainable soil management techniques, such as cover cropping, mulching, and contour planting, promote soil health, reduce erosion, and enhance nutrient cycling in agricultural landscapes.

### 2. Loss of Organic Matter:
- Continuous avocado cultivation without adequate soil conservation measures leads to the loss of organic matter and microbial diversity in the soil. Soil degradation diminishes the capacity of soils to support healthy plant growth and resilience to environmental stressors.

- Implementing soil conservation practices and adopting agroecological approaches help replenish organic matter, improve soil structure, and sustain long-term agricultural productivity.

## Climate Change Impacts

### 1. Greenhouse Gas Emissions:
- Agricultural activities associated with avocado farming, such as land clearing, fertilizer application, and transportation, contribute to greenhouse gas emissions. Carbon dioxide ($CO_2$), methane ($CH_4$), and nitrous oxide ($N_2O$) emissions from agricultural operations contribute to global warming and climate variability.
- Mitigating greenhouse gas emissions through carbon sequestration, renewable energy adoption, and agroforestry integration supports climate resilience and reduces the carbon footprint of avocado production systems.

### 2. Adaptation Strategies:
- Climate change exacerbates environmental risks and uncertainties for avocado farmers,

including shifts in precipitation patterns, temperature extremes, and pest outbreaks. Implementing climate-smart agriculture practices, such as water-efficient irrigation, drought-resistant cultivars, and climate-resilient farming systems, enhances adaptive capacity and sustainability in avocado production.
- Collaborative efforts among farmers, researchers, and policymakers are essential to develop and implement adaptation strategies that safeguard agricultural livelihoods and ecosystems amidst climate uncertainty.

## Conservation and Sustainable Practices

### 1. Certification and Standards:
- Adoption of certification schemes, such as organic certification and Fair Trade certification, promotes sustainable avocado farming practices. These standards emphasize environmental stewardship, social responsibility, and economic viability, fostering transparency and consumer trust in avocado products.

- Compliance with certification requirements encourages farmers to implement environmentally friendly practices, conserve natural resources, and minimize negative impacts on biodiversity and ecosystems.

2. **Ecosystem Restoration:**
    - Restoration initiatives, including reforestation, habitat conservation, and ecological restoration projects, mitigate the environmental footprint of avocado farming. Restoring degraded landscapes enhances biodiversity, protects watershed integrity, and provides ecosystem services crucial for agricultural sustainability.
    - Collaborative conservation efforts involving government agencies, non-governmental organizations (NGOs), and local communities support landscape-scale restoration and promote resilient agroecosystems.

The environmental impact of avocado farming in regions like Michoacán underscores the importance of adopting sustainable practices and mitigating ecological risks to ensure the long-term viability of agricultural systems. Balancing economic prosperity with environmental stewardship requires innovation, collaboration, and commitment to conservation principles. By integrating conservation practices, enhancing water resource management, promoting soil health, and addressing climate change challenges, stakeholders can contribute to a resilient and sustainable avocado industry that benefits ecosystems, communities, and global food security.

## Sustainable Practices and Future Outlook

The avocado industry in Michoacán faces increasing pressure to adopt sustainable practices that balance economic growth with environmental stewardship and social responsibility. As global demand for avocados continues to rise, stakeholders are exploring innovative approaches to ensure the long-term viability and resilience of avocado production in the region. This section examines sustainable practices currently being implemented and outlines the future outlook for sustainable agriculture in Michoacán's avocado industry.

# Current Sustainable Practices

## Conservation of Natural Resources

### 1. Water Management:
- Sustainable water management practices, such as drip irrigation and water recycling systems, help optimize water use efficiency in avocado orchards. These practices mitigate water scarcity risks and reduce environmental impact.
- Investments in water conservation technologies and infrastructure support sustainable agriculture and ensure reliable water supply for avocado cultivation.

### 2. Soil Health and Fertility:
- Conservation tillage and cover cropping techniques promote soil health and fertility, reducing erosion and nutrient depletion in avocado orchards. Organic soil amendments and composting enhance soil structure and support sustainable crop production.
- Soil conservation practices contribute to long-term sustainability, preserving natural habitats and enhancing ecosystem services essential for agricultural productivity.

**Biodiversity Conservation**

**1. Forest Protection:**
- Initiatives to protect and restore native forests adjacent to avocado plantations mitigate deforestation and habitat loss. Conservation easements and reforestation programs contribute to biodiversity conservation and ecosystem resilience.
- Sustainable land use practices integrate avocado farming with forest stewardship, promoting biodiversity corridors and preserving critical habitats for wildlife.

**2. Pollinator Habitat:**
- Establishment of pollinator-friendly habitats and integrated pest management (IPM) practices enhance biodiversity in avocado orchards. Native plantings and habitat restoration initiatives support pollinator populations essential for fruit set and crop yield.
- Conservation of pollinator habitat strengthens ecological resilience and enhances ecosystem services, promoting

natural pest control and reducing reliance on chemical inputs.

## Social Responsibility and Community Engagement

### 1. Labor Practices:
- Adherence to fair labor standards and ethical recruitment practices ensures safe working conditions and fair wages for farm workers in the avocado industry. Training programs and capacity-building initiatives promote worker empowerment and professional development.
Socially responsible sourcing practices foster community trust and strengthen partnerships between growers, workers, and local stakeholders.

### 2. Community Development:
- Investment in community infrastructure, healthcare facilities, and educational opportunities supports sustainable development goals in avocado-growing regions. Corporate social responsibility (CSR) initiatives contribute to poverty alleviation and social equity.
- Collaboration with local communities and indigenous groups promotes inclusive

growth and cultural preservation, enhancing social cohesion and resilience.

## Future Outlook

### Innovation and Technological Advancements

**1. Precision Agriculture:**
- Integration of digital technologies, data analytics, and remote sensing tools enables precision agriculture practices in avocado production. Real-time monitoring of soil health, crop nutrition, and weather conditions optimizes resource allocation and enhances farm productivity.
- Adoption of smart farming technologies improves decision-making processes, reduces environmental footprint, and enhances crop resilience to climate variability.

**2. Climate Resilience:**
- Research and development initiatives focus on breeding resilient avocado varieties and adapting farming practices to climate change

impacts. Climate-smart agriculture strategies include drought-tolerant cultivars and agroforestry systems that enhance farm resilience.
- Investment in climate adaptation measures and risk management strategies prepares avocado growers for extreme weather events and shifting climate patterns, ensuring sustainable production and food security.

## Sustainable Supply Chain Management

### 1. Traceability and Certification:
- Implementation of blockchain technology and supply chain transparency initiatives improves traceability and certification of sustainably sourced avocados. Verification of environmental, social, and ethical standards enhances market access and consumer confidence.
- Collaboration with certification bodies and industry stakeholders promotes adherence to international sustainability standards and best practices, fostering market differentiation and premium pricing opportunities.

**2. Circular Economy Practices:**
- Adoption of circular economy principles in avocado processing and waste management reduces resource consumption and promotes resource efficiency. Recycling of organic waste into compost and bioenergy supports closed-loop systems and reduces environmental impact.
- Circular economy strategies minimize waste generation, optimize resource utilization, and mitigate greenhouse gas emissions, aligning with global sustainability goals and corporate environmental commitments.

## Policy and Regulatory Support

**1. Policy Alignment:**
- Alignment of national policies and regulatory frameworks with international sustainability standards promotes responsible avocado production practices. Incentives for sustainable agriculture and enforcement of environmental regulations enhance compliance and accountability.
- Stakeholder engagement and multi-sectoral partnerships facilitate policy dialogue and

promote collaborative governance approaches to sustainable development.

2. **Market Demand and Consumer Awareness:**
- Growing consumer demand for ethically sourced and sustainably produced avocados drives market transformation and industry innovation. Consumer education initiatives and eco-labeling schemes empower consumers to make informed purchasing decisions.
- Market-driven sustainability initiatives create market opportunities for sustainable avocado growers, incentivizing industry-wide adoption of best practices and driving positive social and environmental outcomes.

The future of Michoacán's avocado industry hinges on its ability to embrace sustainable practices that balance economic prosperity with environmental integrity and social equity. By investing in innovation, fostering community engagement, and strengthening regulatory frameworks, stakeholders can promote a resilient and sustainable avocado industry. Collaborative efforts across sectors and proactive leadership in sustainability will ensure that Michoacán continues to thrive as a global leader in avocado production, meeting the demands of today's consumers while safeguarding the resources for future generations.

# Chapter 8: Solutions and Future Directions

## Strengthening Security and Oversight

Ensuring the security and oversight of Michoacán's avocado industry is paramount to its sustainable development and global competitiveness. This chapter explores comprehensive solutions and future directions aimed at enhancing security measures, improving regulatory oversight, and mitigating risks associated with criminal activities and cartel influence in the avocado trade.

## Enhanced Security Measures

### Law Enforcement Collaboration

1. **Interagency Coordination:**
   - Strengthening collaboration between local, state, and federal law enforcement agencies is essential to combatting organized crime

and ensuring the safety of avocado industry stakeholders.
- Joint task forces and intelligence-sharing initiatives improve responsiveness to security threats and enhance operational effectiveness in crime prevention and detection.

**2. Capacity Building:**
- Investing in law enforcement training programs and professional development enhances the capabilities of security forces in Michoacán. Specialized training in anti-extortion tactics, hostage negotiation, and crisis management prepares law enforcement officers to effectively address security challenges.
- Technical assistance and equipment provision, including surveillance technology and communication systems, bolster law enforcement capabilities and support proactive crime prevention strategies.

## Community Engagement and Empowerment

**1. Community Policing:**

- Promoting community-based policing initiatives empowers local residents to collaborate with law enforcement agencies in identifying criminal activities and reporting security threats.
- Establishing neighborhood watch programs and citizen patrols fosters community resilience and enhances public safety through collective action and vigilance.

**2. Social Programs and Youth Engagement:**
- Investing in youth development programs, vocational training, and educational opportunities reduces susceptibility to recruitment by criminal organizations.
- Social intervention initiatives, including sports clubs, cultural activities, and job placement services, provide alternatives to illicit activities and promote positive youth engagement in community-building efforts.

## Regulatory Oversight and Compliance

**Strengthening Regulatory Frameworks**

1. **Enforcement of Environmental Regulations:**
   - Enhancing regulatory enforcement mechanisms ensures compliance with environmental laws and mitigates environmental degradation associated with avocado cultivation.
   - Monitoring and inspection protocols verify adherence to sustainable farming practices, including water management, soil conservation, and biodiversity protection.

2. **Traceability and Certification:**
   - Implementing robust traceability systems and certification standards enhances transparency and accountability throughout the avocado supply chain.
   - Certification programs, such as organic certification and fair trade practices, certify sustainably produced avocados and provide market incentives for growers adhering to ethical and environmental standards.

**Public-Private Partnerships**

**1. Industry Collaboration:**

- Collaborating with industry associations, private companies, and civil society organizations promotes collective action in promoting ethical business practices and sustainable development.
- Public-private partnerships facilitate knowledge sharing, resource mobilization, and joint initiatives aimed at strengthening supply chain integrity and promoting responsible business conduct.

**2. Stakeholder Engagement:**
- Engaging stakeholders, including avocado growers, exporters, retailers, and consumers, in dialogue and decision-making processes fosters consensus-building and promotes shared responsibility for industry sustainability.
- Multi-stakeholder platforms and advisory committees provide opportunities for collaboration on policy development, risk management, and innovation in avocado production and trade.

## Future Directions

## Innovation and Technology Integration

### 1. Digital Solutions:
- Harnessing digital technologies, such as blockchain, IoT (Internet of Things), and satellite imagery, enhances transparency, efficiency, and accountability in avocado production and supply chain management.
- Real-time data analytics and predictive modeling support decision-making processes, optimize resource allocation, and mitigate operational risks in agricultural production.

### 2. Climate Resilience and Sustainable Practices:
- Investing in climate-resilient agriculture practices, including climate-smart farming techniques and drought-resistant crop varieties, strengthens the resilience of avocado production systems to climate change impacts.
- Research and development initiatives focus on sustainable land use planning, water conservation strategies, and ecosystem restoration efforts to mitigate environmental risks and enhance agricultural sustainability.

## Policy Innovation and Governance

**1. Policy Reform:**
- Advocating for policy reforms, including legislative amendments and regulatory updates, supports adaptive governance frameworks and promotes regulatory coherence in avocado production and trade.
- Policy innovation initiatives address emerging challenges, promote inclusive growth, and foster sustainable development outcomes aligned with national and international sustainability goals.

**2. Global Collaboration**Engaging in international partnerships and alliances promotes best practices exchange, knowledge sharing, and capacity-building initiatives in avocado production and supply chain management.
   - Global collaboration initiatives strengthen market access, enhance export competitiveness, and promote sustainable development practices across global avocado markets.

Strengthening security and oversight measures in Michoacán's avocado industry requires a comprehensive approach that integrates law enforcement, regulatory oversight, community engagement, and technological innovation. By enhancing security capabilities, improving regulatory compliance, and fostering collaborative partnerships, stakeholders can mitigate risks associated with criminal activities and cartel influence while promoting sustainable development and resilience in the avocado industry. Continued commitment to innovative solutions and future-oriented strategies will ensure a safe, transparent, and sustainable avocado trade that benefits local communities, supports economic growth, and preserves environmental integrity for future generations.

## Technological Innovations in Agriculture and Monitoring

Technological advancements play a pivotal role in transforming agriculture practices in Michoacán's avocado industry, enhancing efficiency, productivity, and sustainability. Innovations in agriculture and monitoring technologies empower growers to optimize resource management, mitigate risks, and adapt to evolving environmental challenges. This section explores key technological innovations shaping avocado cultivation in

Michoacán, highlighting their impact on farm operations, environmental stewardship, and future prospects.

## Precision Agriculture

Precision agriculture revolutionizes farming practices by integrating digital technologies, data analytics, and geospatial tools to optimize resource use and decision-making processes. In Michoacán's avocado orchards, precision agriculture techniques are transforming how farmers manage crop health, irrigation, and soil fertility.

1. **Remote Sensing and GIS (Geographic Information System):**
    - Remote sensing technologies, including satellite imagery and drones, provide real-time data on crop health, water stress, and nutrient deficiencies. GIS software enables spatial analysis and mapping of farm landscapes, facilitating targeted interventions and precision application of inputs.
    - Monitoring avocado orchards from above allows farmers to detect early signs of disease outbreaks, pest infestations, or

environmental stressors, enabling timely interventions to minimize crop losses and optimize yields.

**2. IoT (Internet of Things) and Sensor Networks:**
- IoT devices and sensor networks installed in avocado orchards collect continuous data on environmental conditions, such as soil moisture, temperature, and humidity levels. Wireless sensors transmit data to centralized platforms for analysis and decision support.
- Real-time monitoring of microclimatic conditions and soil parameters enables adaptive irrigation scheduling and precision nutrient management, promoting efficient resource use and reducing environmental impact.

## Automated Farming Technologies

Automation and robotics are revolutionizing farm operations in Michoacán, enhancing productivity, labor efficiency, and operational safety in avocado cultivation.

**1. Robotic Harvesting Systems:**

- Robotic harvesters equipped with computer vision and AI technologies selectively harvest ripe avocados from trees, minimizing damage and optimizing fruit quality. Automated sorting and packing systems streamline post-harvest handling processes, reducing labor costs and improving market readiness.
- Robotics alleviate dependency on manual labor, addressing labor shortages and seasonal fluctuations while enhancing harvesting precision and throughput in large-scale avocado plantations.

**2. Autonomous Vehicles and Equipment:**
- Autonomous tractors and machinery automate field operations, such as soil preparation, planting, and orchard maintenance tasks. GPS-guided navigation systems enable precise row spacing and application of agricultural inputs, optimizing operational efficiency and reducing input costs.
- Integration of autonomous technologies enhances operational safety and worker welfare by minimizing exposure to hazardous conditions and repetitive tasks,

promoting sustainable workforce management practices.

## Data-driven Decision Support Systems

Advanced analytics and machine learning algorithms empower farmers and agronomists to make data-driven decisions and optimize agricultural practices in Michoacán's avocado industry.

1. **Predictive Analytics and Modeling:**
   - Predictive models leverage historical data and environmental variables to forecast crop yields, disease outbreaks, and optimal harvest timings. Machine learning algorithms analyze complex datasets to identify patterns and correlations, guiding proactive management strategies.
   - Decision support systems enable scenario planning and risk assessment, enhancing resilience to climate variability and market fluctuations while maximizing profitability and sustainability.

2. **Cloud-based Farm Management Platforms:**
    - Cloud-based platforms centralize farm data and operational workflows, facilitating collaborative planning and real-time monitoring across avocado supply chains. Mobile applications provide growers with remote access to critical information and actionable insights.
    - Digital connectivity improves communication and transparency among stakeholders, from growers and suppliers to retailers and consumers, fostering traceability and accountability throughout the avocado production cycle.

#### Sustainable Agriculture Practices

Technological innovations support the adoption of sustainable agriculture practices in Michoacán, promoting environmental stewardship and resource efficiency across avocado farms.

1. Precision Water and Nutrient Management:
    - Smart irrigation systems and nutrient delivery systems optimize water and fertilizer use based on real-time crop needs and soil conditions. Water sensors and soil

moisture probes enable precise irrigation scheduling, reducing water wastage and nutrient runoff.
- Sustainable farming practices minimize environmental impact while enhancing soil health and fertility, ensuring long-term sustainability of avocado production in Michoacán.

**2. Climate-smart Farming Techniques:**
- Climate-resilient farming strategies, such as agroforestry and cover cropping, enhance biodiversity and ecosystem resilience in avocado orchards. Integration of shade trees and biodiversity corridors mitigate climate risks and support natural pest control.
- Adoption of climate-smart practices improves farm productivity and profitability while mitigating greenhouse gas emissions and enhancing carbon sequestration, contributing to climate change mitigation efforts.

## Future Prospects

The future of technological innovations in Michoacán's avocado industry holds promising opportunities for sustainable growth, resilience, and global competitiveness. Continued investment in research and development, collaboration across sectors, and policy support are essential to harnessing the full potential of technology in avocado cultivation.

1. **Emerging Technologies:**
   - Emerging technologies, such as blockchain for supply chain transparency and gene editing for crop improvement, offer new avenues for enhancing sustainability and quality assurance in avocado production.
   - Integration of AI-driven analytics and robotic systems will further optimize farm operations, enhance productivity, and mitigate operational risks in a dynamic agricultural landscape.

2. **Collaborative Innovation:**
   - Industry partnerships and knowledge exchange initiatives promote innovation diffusion and technology transfer among avocado growers, research institutions, and technology providers.
   - Collaboration with academia, government agencies, and international organizations facilitates adaptive research and

capacity-building programs, addressing local challenges and global agricultural trends.

3. **Policy and Regulatory Frameworks:**
   - Supportive policy frameworks and regulatory incentives encourage the adoption of sustainable agriculture practices and technological innovations in Michoacán's avocado industry.
   - Policy coherence and institutional support strengthen resilience to external shocks, promote market access, and ensure compliance with international sustainability standards, enhancing the region's reputation as a responsible avocado supplier.

Technological innovations are pivotal in shaping the future of agriculture in Michoacán, enabling avocado growers to navigate complex challenges while seizing opportunities for sustainable growth and resilience. By harnessing the transformative power of precision agriculture, automation, data analytics, and sustainable practices, Michoacán's avocado industry can achieve sustainable development goals, enhance environmental stewardship, and meet the demands of a rapidly evolving global market. Continued investment in technological advancements and collaborative partnerships will pave the way for a prosperous and sustainable future for avocado cultivation in Michoacán.

## International Cooperation and Policy Recommendations

The avocado industry in Michoacán, Mexico, operates within a complex web of international trade relations, regulatory frameworks, and sustainability challenges. As global demand for avocados grows, international cooperation becomes increasingly crucial in addressing shared concerns related to environmental conservation, labor rights, market stability, and sustainable development. This section explores the importance of international cooperation in the avocado industry and proposes policy recommendations to foster collaboration, enhance sustainability, and promote equitable growth.

## Importance of International Cooperation

## Trade Relations and Market Access

**1. Bilateral Agreements:**
- Bilateral trade agreements between Mexico and importing countries, particularly the United States, govern avocado exports and market access. These agreements establish tariffs, quotas, and sanitary regulations that influence trade flows and economic stability.
- Negotiations on market access and trade barriers aim to facilitate smoother avocado exports, reduce tariff barriers, and ensure compliance with international food safety standards.

**2. Multilateral Trade Organizations:**
- Participation in multilateral trade organizations such as the World Trade Organization (WTO) and regional economic blocs strengthens Mexico's position in global trade negotiations. Advocacy for fair trade practices and dispute resolution mechanisms safeguards avocado producers' interests.
- Collaboration with international organizations promotes transparency, fosters regulatory coherence, and enhances market predictability for avocado exporters.

# Environmental Sustainability and Conservation

## 1. Climate Change Mitigation:
- International cooperation on climate change mitigation strategies supports avocado-producing regions in adapting to climate variability and reducing greenhouse gas emissions. Knowledge-sharing on sustainable agriculture practices and climate-smart technologies enhances farm resilience.
- Commitments to global climate agreements, such as the Paris Agreement, encourage countries to implement sustainable land use practices and promote reforestation efforts in avocado-growing areas.

## 2. Biodiversity Conservation:
- Collaboration on biodiversity conservation initiatives protects natural habitats and promotes ecosystem resilience in avocado-producing regions. Joint research projects, conservation partnerships, and habitat restoration programs mitigate deforestation and habitat loss.
- Integration of biodiversity considerations into agricultural policies and practices

ensures the long-term viability of avocado farming while preserving critical ecosystems and wildlife habitats.

## Social Responsibility and Labor Rights

### 1. Labor Standards and Human Rights:
- International cooperation on labor standards and human rights promotes fair labor practices and social responsibility in the avocado industry. Dialogue with international labor organizations and civil society groups enhances worker protections and supports ethical recruitment practices.
- Implementation of international labor conventions and corporate social responsibility (CSR) initiatives strengthens accountability, fosters inclusive growth, and empowers vulnerable communities in avocado-producing regions.

### 2. Community Development:
- Partnerships with international development agencies and non-governmental organizations (NGOs) facilitate community development projects in avocado-growing communities. Investments in education,

healthcare, and infrastructure promote socio-economic empowerment and reduce inequality.
- Capacity-building programs and technical assistance enhance local governance capabilities, promote inclusive decision-making processes, and strengthen resilience to socio-economic shocks.

## Policy Recommendations

### Strengthening Regulatory Frameworks

### 1. Harmonization of Standards:
- Harmonize avocado quality and safety standards across exporting and importing countries to streamline trade processes and ensure consistent product quality. Mutual recognition agreements on certification and inspection protocols enhance market access and consumer confidence.
- Establish a framework for regulatory cooperation and information exchange to address emerging food safety concerns, pest management strategies, and technological innovations in avocado production.

2. **Enforcement of Environmental Regulations:**
   - Strengthen enforcement mechanisms for environmental regulations and land use policies to combat illegal deforestation, land degradation, and biodiversity loss associated with avocado cultivation. Implement monitoring systems and satellite imaging technologies to track land-use changes and enforce compliance.
   - Incentivize sustainable land management practices through financial incentives, tax credits, and certification schemes that reward environmental stewardship and promote ecosystem conservation.

## Promoting Sustainable Supply Chains

1. **Supply Chain Transparency:**
   - Enhance supply chain transparency through digital technologies, blockchain solutions, and traceability systems to verify the origin and sustainability credentials of avocados. Promote eco-labeling and certification programs that inform consumers about sustainable production practices.

- Foster collaboration among stakeholders along the avocado supply chain, including growers, processors, retailers, and consumers, to promote responsible sourcing practices and reduce environmental impact.

2. **Investment in Research and Innovation:**
   - Invest in research and development initiatives that advance sustainable agriculture technologies, climate-resilient crop varieties, and efficient water management strategies in avocado farming. Support innovation hubs and agricultural extension services to disseminate best practices and enhance farm productivity.
   - Foster public-private partnerships and international research collaborations to accelerate technological innovation, address agronomic challenges, and promote sustainable intensification in avocado production.

## Empowering Stakeholder Engagement

1. **Stakeholder Dialogue and Engagement:**
   - Facilitate inclusive stakeholder dialogue and multi-sectoral partnerships to address

shared challenges and opportunities in the avocado industry. Establish platforms for knowledge-sharing, policy dialogue, and collaborative decision-making among governments, businesses, academia, and civil society.
- Promote participatory governance models that prioritize local knowledge, cultural values, and community-driven solutions to sustainable development in avocado-producing regions.

## 2. Capacity Building and Institutional Strengthening:
- Build institutional capacity and regulatory frameworks that support sustainable avocado production and promote socio-economic development in rural communities. Provide technical assistance, training programs, and financial support to strengthen local governance structures and agricultural cooperatives.
- Empower small-scale farmers, indigenous communities, and women entrepreneurs in the avocado sector through targeted capacity-building initiatives, access to market information, and inclusive business

models that promote economic empowerment and social inclusion.

International cooperation is indispensable in shaping the future of Michoacán's avocado industry, fostering sustainable development, and addressing global challenges. By promoting dialogue, enhancing regulatory frameworks, and investing in sustainable practices, stakeholders can build resilient avocado supply chains, protect natural resources, and promote inclusive growth. Policy recommendations outlined above provide a roadmap for collaborative action, guiding efforts to achieve sustainable agriculture, environmental conservation, and socio-economic progress in avocado-producing regions. Through collective commitment and partnership, the avocado industry can thrive in a globally interconnected marketplace while safeguarding the environment and improving livelihoods for present and future generations.

# Chapter 9: Consumer Awareness

## Understanding the Journey of Your Avocado

In today's interconnected world, consumers are increasingly interested in understanding the origins and sustainability practices behind the products they purchase, including avocados. This chapter explores the journey of avocados from farm to table, highlighting the complexities of their production, distribution, and environmental impact. By understanding this journey, consumers can make informed choices that support sustainable practices and promote transparency in the avocado industry.

## The Global Avocado Supply Chain

1. **Farm Production:**
   - Avocados are primarily grown in regions with suitable climates and soil conditions, such as Michoacán, Mexico, and various

regions in California, Peru, and other tropical and subtropical areas.
- Farmers cultivate avocado trees, carefully managing orchards to ensure optimal growth and fruit quality. Sustainable farming practices, including water management and soil conservation, play a crucial role in minimizing environmental impact.

2. **Harvesting and Processing:**
- Avocado harvesting involves careful hand-picking of ripe fruits to prevent damage. Harvested avocados are transported to packing facilities where they undergo sorting, washing, and grading processes.
- Quality control measures, including inspection for size, ripeness, and defects, ensure that only high-quality avocados reach consumers. Processing facilities adhere to food safety standards to maintain product integrity.

3. **Packaging and Distribution:**
- After processing, avocados are packaged in containers suitable for transportation. Cold storage facilities maintain optimal temperature and humidity levels to extend

shelf life and preserve freshness during distribution.
- Distribution networks transport avocados across national and international borders, connecting producers with consumers in diverse markets. Efficient logistics and supply chain management support timely delivery and reduce food waste.

## Environmental and Social Considerations

**1. Sustainable Practices:**
- Consumers are increasingly concerned about the environmental impact of avocado production. Sustainable farming practices, such as organic cultivation, water conservation, and biodiversity conservation, mitigate environmental degradation.
- Certifications and eco-labels, such as Fair Trade and Rainforest Alliance, indicate adherence to sustainable practices and ethical standards. Consumers can choose certified avocados to support responsible farming and environmental stewardship.

**2. Social Responsibility:**

- Ethical sourcing practices prioritize fair labor standards, worker welfare, and community development in avocado-growing regions. Companies that support social initiatives and community empowerment contribute to sustainable livelihoods.
- Transparency in supply chains enables consumers to trace the origins of avocados and verify compliance with social and ethical standards. Engagement with certified growers promotes accountability and ethical consumerism.

## Making Informed Choices

### 1. Consumer Education:
- Educating consumers about the nutritional benefits, culinary versatility, and sustainable attributes of avocados enhances awareness and appreciation for this popular fruit.
- Resources such as product labels, websites, and educational campaigns provide information on avocado origins, production methods, and sustainability practices. Accessible information empowers consumers to make informed purchasing decisions.

## 2. Supporting Sustainable Brands:
- Choosing brands and retailers committed to sustainability and ethical sourcing practices encourages industry-wide adoption of responsible behaviors.
- Consumer demand for sustainable avocados drives market incentives for producers to invest in environmental stewardship and social responsibility. Support for sustainable brands promotes market transparency and accountability.

Understanding the journey of avocados from farm to table empowers consumers to support sustainable practices and make environmentally conscious choices. By advocating for transparency, ethical sourcing, and responsible consumption, consumers play a pivotal role in promoting sustainability in the avocado industry. Continued engagement, education, and collaboration among stakeholders contribute to a more resilient and equitable global food system, ensuring that future generations can enjoy avocados while safeguarding the planet and supporting thriving communities.

# Supporting Ethical and Sustainable Practices

Ethical and sustainable practices are critical pillars for ensuring the long-term viability, environmental integrity, and social responsibility of the avocado industry in Michoacán, Mexico. As global demand for avocados continues to rise, stakeholders across the supply chain must prioritize ethical considerations and adopt sustainable agricultural practices that promote environmental stewardship, uphold labor rights, and benefit local communities. This section explores strategies to support ethical and sustainable practices in the avocado industry, emphasizing the importance of collaboration, transparency, and responsible business conduct.

## Environmental Sustainability

**1. Regenerative Agriculture:**
- Promote regenerative farming practices that enhance soil health, biodiversity, and ecosystem resilience in avocado orchards. Techniques such as cover cropping, crop rotation, and agroforestry systems restore

soil fertility, sequester carbon, and reduce reliance on synthetic inputs.
- Implement integrated pest management (IPM) strategies to minimize chemical pesticide use and promote natural pest control methods. Biological pest controls and companion planting contribute to ecological balance and support sustainable crop production.

**2. Water Conservation:**
- Adopt water-efficient irrigation technologies, such as drip irrigation and micro-sprinklers, to optimize water use efficiency in avocado farming. Capture and reuse rainwater and irrigation runoff to mitigate water scarcity risks and support sustainable water management practices.
- Implement soil moisture monitoring systems and precision irrigation techniques to minimize water wastage and ensure adequate hydration for avocado trees throughout their growth cycle.

**3. Climate Resilience:**
- Develop climate-resilient avocado cultivars and adaptive farming practices that withstand climate variability and extreme

weather events. Research and innovation in crop breeding, genetic diversity conservation, and climate-smart agriculture enhance farm resilience and food security.
- Integrate climate adaptation strategies, such as mulching, windbreaks, and shade management, to mitigate heat stress and optimize growing conditions for avocado trees in changing climatic conditions.

## Social Responsibility and Labor Rights

### 1. Fair Labor Practices:
- Ensure adherence to fair labor standards, occupational safety regulations, and ethical recruitment practices in avocado production. Provide training programs, worker empowerment initiatives, and safe working conditions to protect the health and well-being of farm workers.
- Promote gender equality and empower women in agriculture through leadership opportunities, vocational training, and access to resources. Support inclusive employment practices and social protection

programs that promote equitable economic opportunities.

2. **Community Engagement:**
   - Engage local communities, indigenous groups, and stakeholders in decision-making processes that impact avocado production and rural development. Foster transparent communication, cultural sensitivity, and collaborative partnerships to build trust and mutual respect.
   - Invest in community development projects, including education, healthcare, and infrastructure improvements, to enhance socio-economic well-being and promote sustainable livelihoods in avocado-growing regions.

# Supply Chain Transparency and Accountability

1. **Traceability and Certification:**
   - Implement robust traceability systems, blockchain technology, and supply chain transparency initiatives to verify the origin and sustainability credentials of avocados. Enable consumers to make informed

purchasing decisions based on ethical sourcing practices and environmental stewardship.
- Obtain certifications, such as Fair Trade, Rainforest Alliance, and organic certifications, that validate compliance with international sustainability standards and promote market differentiation for ethically sourced avocados.

**2. Supplier Codes of Conduct:**
- Establish supplier codes of conduct and responsible sourcing policies that prioritize ethical business practices, human rights, and environmental conservation throughout the avocado supply chain. Conduct regular audits and assessments to monitor compliance and address non-compliance issues promptly.
- Collaborate with suppliers, growers, and stakeholders to implement best practices, share knowledge, and promote continuous improvement in ethical sourcing and sustainable supply chain management.

## Policy and Advocacy

1. **Advocacy for Sustainable Agriculture:**
   - Advocate for policies and regulatory frameworks that support sustainable agriculture, biodiversity conservation, and environmental protection in avocado-producing regions. Engage policymakers, government agencies, and civil society organizations in shaping policy priorities and legislative reforms.
   - Participate in industry associations, working groups, and multi-stakeholder platforms to drive collective action, share best practices, and advocate for industry-wide standards that prioritize sustainability and ethical business conduct.

2. **Capacity Building and Training:**
   - Provide capacity-building programs, technical assistance, and training workshops to empower avocado growers and industry stakeholders with the knowledge and skills needed to adopt sustainable practices. Promote innovation, research collaboration, and knowledge exchange to foster continuous learning and improvement.
   - Support educational initiatives, research partnerships, and extension services that promote sustainable agriculture,

environmental stewardship, and socio-economic development in avocado-producing communities.

Supporting ethical and sustainable practices in the avocado industry requires concerted efforts from all stakeholders, including growers, processors, retailers, consumers, and policymakers. By prioritizing environmental sustainability, promoting social responsibility, and ensuring supply chain transparency, stakeholders can build a resilient and inclusive avocado industry that benefits both people and the planet. Continued collaboration, innovation, and advocacy for ethical business practices will pave the way for a sustainable future where avocado production contributes positively to global food security, environmental conservation, and socio-economic development.

## Making Informed Choices as a Consumer

Consumers play a pivotal role in shaping the sustainability and ethical practices of the avocado industry in Michoacán and beyond. Making informed choices empowers consumers to support responsible avocado production, promote environmental stewardship, and uphold social responsibility. This section explores key considerations for consumers when purchasing avocados, including sustainability certifications, ethical sourcing practices, and the impact of consumer behavior on the avocado supply chain.

## Understanding Sustainability Certifications

**1. Certification Programs:**
- Look for reputable sustainability certifications such as Rainforest Alliance, Fair Trade, or USDA Organic labels on avocado packaging. These certifications indicate compliance with environmental, social, and ethical standards in avocado production.
- Certification programs promote sustainable farming practices, fair labor conditions, and biodiversity conservation in avocado-growing regions. They provide assurance that avocados are produced responsibly and contribute positively to communities and ecosystems.

2. **Eco-labeling and Transparency:**
    - Choose avocados with eco-labels or transparency initiatives that disclose information about the origin, farming practices, and supply chain traceability. Transparency enables consumers to make informed decisions based on ethical considerations and sustainability principles.
    - Support brands and retailers committed to supply chain transparency, ethical sourcing, and environmental stewardship. Engage with companies that prioritize social responsibility and demonstrate accountability in their avocado sourcing practices.

## Ethical Sourcing Practices

### 1. Labor Rights and Fair Trade:
- Prioritize avocados from producers and brands that uphold fair labor standards and ethical sourcing practices. Look for certifications that ensure workers receive fair wages, safe working conditions, and opportunities for professional development.

- Support fair trade initiatives that empower small-scale farmers, promote gender equality, and foster community development in avocado-growing communities. Ethical sourcing practices contribute to poverty alleviation and social equity in rural areas.

## 2. Environmental Impact:
- Consider the environmental impact of avocado production practices, such as water use efficiency, pesticide management, and habitat conservation. Choose avocados from farms that implement sustainable agriculture techniques and minimize ecological footprint.
- Opt for organic or sustainably grown avocados that prioritize soil health, biodiversity conservation, and natural resource management. Sustainable farming practices reduce chemical inputs, promote ecosystem resilience, and protect wildlife habitats.

# Consumer Behavior and Supply Chain Impact

### 1. Demand for Sustainable Products:

- Influence the avocado supply chain by expressing preferences for sustainably produced avocados. Consumer demand drives market incentives for growers and suppliers to adopt sustainable practices and improve supply chain transparency.
- Participate in consumer advocacy campaigns, petitions, and initiatives that promote sustainability standards and ethical sourcing in the avocado industry. Advocate for corporate responsibility and accountability in supply chain management.

2. **Educational Resources and Awareness:**
   - Stay informed about issues affecting the avocado industry, including environmental conservation, labor rights, and community impacts. Educate yourself through reputable sources, consumer guides, and sustainability reports from industry organizations.
   - Engage with educational programs, workshops, and online resources that highlight the importance of sustainable consumption and responsible purchasing decisions. Empower yourself to make choices aligned with your values and sustainability goals.

## Promoting Positive Change

**1. Supporting Sustainable Brands:**
- Patronize brands and retailers committed to sustainable sourcing practices and ethical business conduct. Reward companies that prioritize environmental stewardship, social responsibility, and transparency in their avocado supply chains.
- Explore alternatives such as local or seasonal avocados that reduce carbon footprint and support regional agriculture. Seek out partnerships with community-supported agriculture (CSA) programs or farmers' markets promoting sustainable food choices.

**2. Feedback and Engagement:**
- Provide feedback to retailers and brands on their avocado sourcing practices and sustainability initiatives. Voice concerns about environmental impacts, labor conditions, and supply chain transparency to encourage continuous improvement and accountability.
- Engage with industry stakeholders, government agencies, and non-governmental organizations (NGOs) advocating for sustainable agriculture policies and

consumer protections. Collaborate to address systemic challenges and promote positive change in the avocado industry.

Making informed choices as a consumer empowers individuals to contribute to a more sustainable and ethical avocado industry in Michoacán and global markets. By supporting sustainable certifications, ethical sourcing practices, and advocating for transparency in the supply chain, consumers can drive positive change and promote responsible avocado production. Each purchasing decision represents an opportunity to prioritize environmental conservation, social equity, and ethical business practices, ensuring a resilient and sustainable future for avocado farming communities and ecosystems worldwide.

# Conclusion

The avocado industry in Michoacán faces a landscape shaped by both challenges and opportunities, reflecting its critical role in global markets and local economies. Throughout this exploration of Michoacán's avocado industry, several key themes have emerged, highlighting the complex interplay of economic, environmental, and social factors that define its trajectory.

## Challenges

**1. Security and Governance Issues:**
- The presence of organized crime and security challenges in avocado-producing regions poses risks to industry stakeholders, including growers, workers, and inspectors. Ensuring safety and security remains a persistent concern requiring coordinated efforts and robust governance.

**2. Environmental Sustainability:**

- Pressures from agricultural expansion, deforestation, and water scarcity underscore the need for sustainable farming practices. Balancing economic growth with environmental stewardship is essential to mitigate ecological impacts and safeguard natural resources.

3. **Social Responsibility and Labor Rights:**
   - Upholding fair labor standards, promoting community development, and addressing socio-economic inequalities are integral to fostering inclusive growth in avocado-growing communities. Enhancing social responsibility across the supply chain is crucial for equitable prosperity.

# Opportunities

1. **Market Growth and Demand:**
   - Increasing global demand for avocados presents opportunities for economic growth and market expansion. Leveraging international trade relations and consumer preferences for sustainably sourced products can drive market differentiation and premium pricing.

2. **Innovation and Technology:**
   - Advances in agricultural technology, precision farming, and climate-resilient practices offer opportunities to enhance productivity and resilience in avocado production. Embracing innovation fosters efficiency, resource optimization, and adaptation to climate change impacts.

3. **International Cooperation and Policy Reform:**
   - Strengthening international cooperation, harmonizing regulatory frameworks, and promoting sustainable development goals are pivotal for shaping a sustainable future for the avocado industry. Policy reforms that support environmental sustainability, labor rights, and ethical business practices can foster positive change.

## Summarizing the Path Forward

The path forward for Michoacán's avocado industry lies in embracing sustainable practices, fostering innovation, and prioritizing social responsibility. By addressing security challenges, enhancing environmental stewardship, and promoting inclusive development, stakeholders can navigate the complexities of global trade while safeguarding the region's natural and cultural heritage.

In conclusion, the avocado industry in Michoacán stands at a crossroads, where proactive measures and collaborative efforts can pave the way for a resilient and sustainable future. By seizing opportunities, mitigating challenges, and advancing collective action, stakeholders can uphold the integrity of avocado production, promote economic prosperity, and nurture thriving communities. Through shared commitment to sustainability and responsible stewardship, Michoacán's "green gold" can continue to enrich global markets while preserving its environmental and social value for generations to come.

## The Future of the Avocado Industry in a Global Context

The avocado industry, centered predominantly in regions like Michoacán, Mexico, faces a dynamic future shaped by evolving consumer preferences, environmental challenges, and international trade dynamics. As global demand for avocados continues to rise, driven by their nutritional benefits and culinary versatility, stakeholders must navigate complex issues related to sustainability, market dynamics, and technological advancements. This section explores the future outlook for the avocado industry in a global context, focusing on key trends, challenges, and opportunities shaping its trajectory.

## Emerging Trends and Market Dynamics

### 1. Rising Consumer Demand:
- Consumer awareness of avocados' health benefits and culinary appeal continues to drive global demand. Growing consumption in North America, Europe, and Asia-Pacific regions expands market opportunities for avocado-producing countries.
- Changing dietary preferences towards plant-based foods and healthy eating habits contribute to sustained growth in avocado consumption. Emerging markets in Asia and the Middle East represent new growth frontiers for avocado exporters.

### 2. Sustainable Sourcing Practices:

- Increasing emphasis on sustainability and ethical sourcing practices reshapes industry standards and consumer expectations. Demand for certified organic, fair trade, and responsibly sourced avocados drives market differentiation and premium pricing.
- Adoption of sustainable agriculture techniques, water conservation practices, and biodiversity initiatives becomes imperative for avocado producers to meet sustainability goals and mitigate environmental impacts.

## Technological Innovations and Agricultural Advancements

### 1. Precision Agriculture:
- Integration of digital technologies, data analytics, and IoT (Internet of Things) solutions revolutionizes avocado farming practices. Precision agriculture enables real-time monitoring of soil health, crop growth, and pest management, optimizing resource use and enhancing farm productivity.
- AI (Artificial Intelligence) and machine learning algorithms provide predictive

analytics and decision support tools for farmers, improving crop yield, quality, and resilience to climate variability.

**2. Climate Resilience and Adaptation:**
- Climate-smart agriculture practices, including drought-tolerant cultivars, agroforestry systems, and water-efficient irrigation methods, help avocado growers adapt to changing climate conditions. Research on resilient crop varieties and sustainable land management practices strengthens farm resilience and food security.
- Collaborative research initiatives and public-private partnerships focus on mitigating climate risks and promoting sustainable development in avocado-producing regions.

## Global Trade Dynamics and Policy Considerations

**1. Trade Agreements and Market Access:**
- Bilateral and multilateral trade agreements influence avocado exports, tariff policies, and market access conditions. Negotiations on

sanitary and phytosanitary standards, trade barriers, and regulatory harmonization impact cross-border trade flows and market stability.
- Advocacy for fair trade practices, tariff reductions, and market diversification strategies supports avocado-producing countries in accessing new markets and enhancing export competitiveness.

## 2. Regulatory Frameworks and Sustainability Standards:
- Alignment with international sustainability standards, such as environmental certifications and labor rights protections, becomes increasingly important for avocado producers. Strengthening regulatory frameworks and enforcement mechanisms ensures compliance with global norms and enhances market credibility.
- Collaboration among governments, industry stakeholders, and civil society organizations promotes policy coherence, transparency, and accountability in avocado supply chains.

# Opportunities for Innovation and Market Expansion

1. **Value-added Products and Market Segmentation:**
   - Innovation in avocado processing, product diversification, and value-added packaging drives market differentiation and consumer engagement. Development of avocado-based cosmetics, functional foods, and culinary products expands market opportunities and enhances product appeal.
   - Targeted marketing campaigns and consumer education initiatives promote the versatility and nutritional benefits of avocados, capturing diverse consumer segments and fostering brand loyalty.

2. **Investment in Infrastructure and Supply Chain Resilience:**
   - Investment in logistics infrastructure, cold chain management, and supply chain resilience strengthens market connectivity and reduces post-harvest losses. Modernization of packing facilities, transportation networks, and distribution channels enhances efficiency and reliability in avocado trade.

- Public-private partnerships and investment in rural infrastructure support inclusive growth, job creation, and economic development in avocado-producing regions, fostering sustainable livelihoods and community resilience.

The future of the avocado industry in a global context hinges on sustainable development, technological innovation, and adaptive strategies to address emerging challenges and opportunities. By embracing sustainable farming practices, leveraging technological advancements, and fostering international cooperation, stakeholders can promote a resilient and thriving avocado industry. Consumer awareness, market demand for ethical products, and policy support for sustainable agriculture will drive industry transformation, ensuring a sustainable supply of avocados while safeguarding environmental integrity and supporting socio-economic development worldwide. Collaborative efforts across sectors and proactive leadership in sustainability will shape a promising future for the avocado industry, meeting the evolving needs of global markets and contributing to a healthier, more sustainable food system.

www.ingramcontent.com/pod-product-compliance
Lightning Source LLC
Chambersburg PA
CBHW071913210526
45479CB00002B/406